Rudy's Red Wagon

COMMUNICATION STRATEGIES IN CONTEMPORARY SOCIETY

Rudy's Red Wagon
COMMUNICATION STRATEGIES IN CONTEMPORARY SOCIETY

Irving J. Rein
NORTHWESTERN UNIVERSITY

Scott, Foresman and Company
GLENVIEW, ILLINOIS   LONDON

ISBN: 0-673-07623-7

Library of Congress Catalog Card Number: 79-166146
Copyright © 1972 by Scott, Foresman and Company, Glenview, Illinois 60025
Philippines Copyright 1972 by Scott, Foresman and Company.
All Rights Reserved.
Printed in the United States of America.
Regional offices of Scott, Foresman and Company are located in Dallas, Oakland,
N.J., Palo Alto, and Tucker, Ga.

ACKNOWLEDGMENTS

2   Used by permission of Volkswagen of America, Inc.
9   From *The Put-On* by Jacob Brackman, published by Henry Regnery Company
    1971. Text copyright © 1967, 1971, originally published in The New Yorker in
    slightly different form. By permission of Bantam Books, Inc.
13 Condensed from an article in the *Chicago Sun-Times*. Reprinted with permission.
37 © 1968 by The New York Times Company. Reprinted by Permission.
60 By permission of The Times Educational Supplement.
81 "Midnight Hour Blues," Words and Music by Leroy Carr. © Copyright 1971 by
    MCA MUSIC, a division of MCA, INC. 445 Park Avenue, New York, N. Y. 10022.
    Used by permission. All rights reserved.
82 © Copyright 1927 by Northern Music Company. Used by permission. All rights
    reserved.
83 "In The Evening (When the Sun Goes Down)," Words and Music by Leroy Carr.
    © Copyright 1935 by MCA MUSIC, a division of MCA, INC., 445 Park Avenue,
    New York, N.Y. 10022. Used by permission. All rights reserved.
84 "Riverside Blues," Words and Music: Thomas Andrew Dorsey © Copyright: 1923 by
    Thomas Andrew Dorsey. Renewed and assigned to Edwin H. Morris & Company, Inc.
    by Thomas Dorsey. Used by permission.
84 "You Don't Know My Min'," Words and Music by Virginia Liston, Samuel Gray,
    and Clarence Williams. © Copyright 1923, 1924 by MCA MUSIC, a division of
    MCA, INC., 445 Park Avenue, New York, N. Y. 10022. Used by permission. All
    rights reserved.
135 "Peace Movement 'Betrayed' by Radicals, Says McGovern," *Chicago Daily News*,
    August 31, 1970. Reprinted by permission of United Press International.
138 "Jesus a Revolutionary," by J. N., from "The People Talk," *Chicago Today*,
    January 2, 1970. Reprinted by permission.

Preface
Number One

This book could not have been written without the cooperation of many people. I am grateful to Northwestern University for providing research money to afford an assistant. Tim Skelly, a college student and artist, did an excellent job in giving perspective and continuity to the book. My students, both undergraduate and graduate, made numerous helpful suggestions, particularly in the area of music and put-ons. My wife, Lynn, typed and edited much of the manuscript and made many valuable additions. The editorial staff at Scott, Foresman was always helpful, and I am grateful to them. And to all the manipulators, shysters, con-artists, and liars about whom this book is written—I am grateful for your transparency.

Since this book is primarily concerned with manipulative strategies, I felt it appropriate to suggest in the title that the basis for these communicative devices lamentably is found early in childhood. Somehow, the image of Rudy, pulling his wagon full of tricks, is more ominous than any other title I could devise. Devious Rudy suggests lost innocence and a bleak future, especially for the many people who may happen to encounter him.

Irving J. Rein
Northwestern University

Contents

Introduction:
Here They Come Again

Who are *they*?

FADE IN:

A moon-faced salesman lights up a twenty-four-inch television screen. He has a gadget that will cut razor-thin slices of tomatoes, cucumbers, and carrots. Readjust the gadget, and whole potatoes become krinkle-cut french fries, and whole lettuce heads become swiftly suitable for chef's salad.

$4.95 Special!
Write—
Salad Klop
Box 123
Zumbrota, Minnesota 55359
Enclose check or money order.

FADE OUT:

Mushy tomatoes, cut fingers, tortured potatoes. "Damn Salad Klop!"

FADE IN:

Between scenes of the severed carcass of *How to Stuff a Wild Bikini*, the fourteenth commercial emerges. A fat, overstuffed, new car (made in Detroit) pulls into a suburban driveway. A fat man steps from the car. A moving van enters the drive of the adjacent, identical-looking house, stops, and deposits a washer, dryer, television set, and refrigerator. While the fat, stunned neighbor watches enviously, the proud multiple-appliance owner pulls up in a new Volkswagen. An oily, sarcastic voice informs the viewer that the fat car cost the fat man as much as the Volkswagen and the additional appliances cost his clever neighbor.

FADE OUT:

Vacant building . . . kid kicking ashcan . . . neon sign flashing "Schlitz" . . . smog.

"There's one more thing about our machines," Feld added. "After the purchase is completed, a recorded message automatically says: 'Thank you very much!' You're lucky if you can get that out of a real, live salesperson nowadays."

--Vending-machine distributor[1]

DOW PREDICTS PRICE BOOSTS Dow Chemical Co. said chemical and plastic prices will head higher in the months ahead because of rising costs. The company did not indicate how much the increases would likely be or when they would occur.[2]

The amount of clanging and banging in American society has reached monumental proportions. Wherever you go, jets streak overhead, cement mixers "puh kaw tuh," and cash registers ring. Automobiles in all sizes and shapes race and roar down involuted and interlaced expressways. Your mind is boggled and your eyes are awed by large, golden McDonald hamburger

signs, spaced every nine and one-half miles between Colonel Sanders
Kentucky Fried Chicken/Midas Muffler/Mr. Donut/Burger King/Zayre/
Firestone Tires/Manpower/Howard Johnson's/Shell/Stuckey's/ Mr. C's
Pizza/39 Flavors/A and W Root Beer/Western Auto Tire Stores . . .

We are surrounded . . . surfeited . . . saturated . . . engulfed. The sounds
and scenes of our society and the furies which produce them impinge,
intrude, inveigle, insidiously infiltrate our consciousness, invade our privacy,
and often infuriate us. And all too frequently it is the intangibility, the
facelessness, of the purveyors of the sound and the suasion and the suavity
that bewilders and enrages us the most.

They are everywhere.

They run real estate firms which frighten whites and sell to blacks at
inflated prices; *they* are bankers who want collateral poor people do not
have; *they* are chain food store operators who put water into their ground
beef; *they* are politicians who promise equality and, after election, cut
education budgets; *they* are college administrators who promise educational
reform and, during summer break, deliver a spongy compromise; *they* are
student leaders who organize marches against university expansion and
disappear when police start cracking heads.

They have power.

This book is about how the powerful and the powerless, through strategy
and tactics at their disposal, battle for the distribution of power.

The number of individuals and groups who are involved in this struggle
is ever growing. From mothers to Baptists, from six-year-olds to homosexuals,
the number keeps increasing and the methods and means continue prolif-
erating. The intent of this book is to analyze some of the means and their
effect in persuading groups of people to espouse one cause or another, or
to take a particular course of action.

What produces the conflicts is that individual consumers of information
feel inadequate in the wake of overpowering communication media. Members
of the group who qualify as *they* consolidate and expand their power, while
the consumer is increasingly unable to control his own destiny. The hardhats,
blacks, students, housewives, and retired see themselves as being incapable of
effectively responding to the messages of the producers of information.
Hence, instead of maintaining a desirable and healthy interaction between
and among groups, the transaction is ever more one-sided and manipulative.
In turn, the consumer becomes frustrated by his inability to use the normal
communication system to redirect his life.

It is inevitable, then, that consumers resort to violence: building
"trashing," hippie beatings, ghetto riots, bombing, killing, suicide. Similarly,
a number of communication strategies, which also are destructive in intent,

intensify. The purpose of such strategies—the put-on and heckling, for example—is manipulation. In the emotional climate which limits meaningful interaction, these strategies are the natural counterpart of physical violence. They are the beginnings of communicative violence.

The emphasis in this book is upon communication forms and strategies which, when their purpose is distorted or exploited, contribute to the weakening of our society's communication systems. These strategies and forms range from obvious weakeners, such as confrontation and stereotyping, to more subtle art forms, such as film, music, and radio. Too frequently, the distortion of these strategies reflects a desire by the producer to limit and control the responses of the consumer. If the consumer does not understand these techniques of manipulation, the communication system is crippled because half of it is missing—the consumer's ability to respond. If the consumer discovers the producer's deception, as he usually does sooner or later, the communication system is weakened still further because of suspicion and mistrust. The negotiations take on the aspects of a game, as both parties abandon open communication in favor of deception and eventual advantage. This sort of manipulation ends in misunderstanding and frustration, which is all too common in our communication system.

This is not to say that these forms of presentation are failures. In the short run, they contribute to the producer's selling his ideas or commodities. The consumer buys the hardtop with the vinyl roof, sells his house in panic, or votes for a man with fewer qualifications. His decisions are based on a potpourri of promises, half-truths, and glitzy presentations. And, in truth, many a customer expects to be deceived. He often feels that he too has the capacity to effect communication and that, when back in power, he can do his own manipulating. There is also a certain joy in the gamesmanship of deception and its full bag of conning tricks. Something about the cleverness of the appliance or automobile salesman is enjoyable and a part of American culture. The good hustle is an art form, and we have learned to appreciate it. In this sense, manipulation is a participatory sport at which most producers and consumers play.

The objection to the deception is that we can do much better in our communication system. A fiercely combative system characterized by a high degree of tension must eventually overload and collapse. There are only so many put-ons that man can sustain before his entire system of interrelationships becomes ambiguous and, ultimately, meaningless. Twenty years ago, the need for a book probing the exploitive, manipulative techniques in our society did not seem as compelling as it does today. Now, new forces and events in our contemporary culture, interacting with new insights into behavioral speech and communication technologies, would seem to make the production of a book of this kind more urgent, more pertinent. Hopefully, in the near future human communication will become more open and straightforward—at which time, perhaps, less games-oriented and more optimistic volumes may be written.

HOW THEY DO IT

SECTION ONE

COME ON IN... I HAVE SOME THINGS TO SHOW YOU.

RING... THEN LEAVE

TODAY THE WORLD!! TOMORROW THE COSMOS!!!

AMONG THE PURE AT HEART, THERE IS AN IMPLICATION THAT STRATEGIES AND TACTICS ARE SOMEHOW DIABOLIC IN INTENT. WHILE ALTERNATING BETWEEN MAINLINING ON HEROIN AND TRIPPING ON LSD, SOME CRAZED YOUNG REVOLUTIONARY IN A CROWDED, FILTHY APARTMENT PLOTS THE MAJOR EVENTS OF OUR TIMES.

WOOG!

HE IS A STRATEGIST!

IT WAS HE WHO STAGED THE 1968 GRANT PARK POLICE RIOT IN CHICAGO; IT WAS HE WHO CONNED THE NATIONAL GUARD INTO KILLING FOUR STUDENTS AT KENT STATE; AND IT WAS HE WHO BOMBED THE MATH BUILDING AT THE UNIVERSITY OF WISCONSIN.

6

THE TERM STRATEGY, HOWEVER, IS NOT REALLY PEJORATIVE. PEOPLE WHO USE STRATEGY ARE NOT INHERENTLY MORE EVIL THAN THOSE WHO ARE "OPEN" AND "INNOCENT." BUT BY MAN'S NATURE, STRATEGY GENERALLY IS MANIPULATIVE, IS CONTINGENT UPON A CERTAIN AMOUNT OF PLANNING, AND ASSUMES AN ADVERSARY. IN THIS SENSE, THE STRATEGIST MAY HAVE AN ADVANTAGE IF THE ADVERSARY OR RECIPIENT OF THE MANIPULATION IS NOT PREPARED.

HELP!! POLICE!!!

SURE, GIMME YOUR DOUGH!

IN THIS SECTION, YOU WILL FIND AN ANALYSIS OF A NUMBER OF STRATEGIES AND TACTICS, VARYING RATHER WIDELY IN THEIR DEGREE OF SOPHISTICATION, BEGINNING WITH THE PUT-ON AND RANGING ON THROUGH CONFRONTATION, REDEFINITION, AND HECKLING THE PROFESSOR.

7

1 The Put-on

The late Senator Everett McKinley Dirksen, in a deep-throated, oily voice, records a sentimental piece on God, country, and marigolds. Yippie leader Abbie Hoffman, during a demonstration at the Pentagon, takes out a ruler and measures the edifice. Tiny Tim, a performer with a falsetto voice and bushy curls, marries on national television. Charlton Heston stars in two motion pictures in which apes take over the world. After class, representatives of the Women's Liberation Front bellicosely accost a professor for calling women "lovely."

"What's the matter with *lovely*?" asks the bewildered professor.

"You're *gorgeous*!" chorus the ladies in reply.

BEATLES' PAUL MCCARTNEY DEAD!

If one linguistic device characterizes the current generation, it is the put-on. The put-on is not mere kidding or joshing, or even lying or telling tall tales. As Jacob Brackman describes it in the *New Yorker*, the put-on occupies "a fuzzy territory between simple leg-pulling and elaborate practical jokes, between pointed lampoon and free-floating spoof." [1] The goal of the kidder is to pass off untruth as truth. Kidding relies on a certain gullibility in the victim; and when the gulled is hooked, the game is over. For the kidder, the joy comes from letting the victim *know* he's been gulled and in watching that realization sink into his consciousness.

In contrast, the victim of the put-on is never really let into the truth—if, indeed, the truth ever existed. The victim is constantly in a state of uncertainty and confusion. A put-on artist does not deal in little pervasive tricks. Rather, he works to develop a sleight-of-hand style that consistently casts into doubt everything he says. Yippie leader Jerry Rubin, a prototype put-on artist, never lets his victims know what his intentions or opinions really are. Rubin is ambiguous, and ambiguity is the essence of the put-on. He arrived to testify at a HUAC (House Committee on Un-American Activities) meeting wearing a Santa Claus suit; and when barred from entering, he replied, "This is how I dress every day. You shouldn't be prejudiced against me because of the way I dress."

HUAC BARS SANTA CLAUS

The put-on is a reaction to what some see as the public apathy to deception that pervades the whole range of modern experience. Teddy Kennedy, inheritor of a legend and presumably a fighter for truth, justice, and beauty, dumps his car and female companion into Chappaquiddick Sound after a party. In *Games People Play*, Eric Berne has written of the hypocrisy and phoniness that saturate the spectrum of American life, from cocktail parties to marital spats. This generation sees itself surrounded by constant manipulation. In NBC news, Spiro T. Agnew, and coffee klatches it sees both insincerity and duplicity. It calls the whole communication system into question. Again, as Jacob Brackman points out:

Paradoxically, this generation--so obsessed with themes of falsehood, phoniness, and hypocrisy--has developed and refined the art of the put-on, as if driven to illustrate that what passes for "truth" and "reality" is often cruelly deceptive. A complex society depends for its survival on some degree of mutual trust among its citizens. But a generation of Americans, having lost all patience with the dishonesties that lubricate social transactions, now appears ready to propagate its own distrust through-out society, to foist upon communication the very cancer it has protested against. The put-on may be a destructive device born out of desperation--a weapon to force people out, through confusion and loss of confidence, toward honesty. Perhaps a hope exists, however dubious, that the debasement of discourse will soon become intolerable--a hope that people, when their legs have been pulled almost to the breaking point, will at last begin to kick.[2]

There are a number of put-on strategies, each with its own peculiarities; but, in some way, each is related to seeing the System as a "giant con game."

The Interview Put-on

The interview is a ready-made setup for the put-on. An interview can be seen as one of the prime weapons of the Establishment. When you try to enter almost any new situation—school, army, or job-hunt—you are interviewed.

There is little question that the interviewer has an easier task than does the hapless slob who is being interviewed.

"How do you see yourself in ten years?"
"What does your father earn a year?"
"Can you manage on $75 a month?"
"How many hours a night do you study?"
"Have you ever had wet dreams?"

The put-on enables the interviewee to break up the incessant questioning by ridiculing the process, and yet at the same time allows him to say some-thing in the process.

CARMICHAEL CALLS FOR
BLACK INVASION OF SCARSDALE !

STUDS TERKEL: "Did the people you knew in the Thirties ever talk about
what happened outside? You know . . . those on
relief . . .?"

SOCIALITE: "I don't think we ever mentioned them. They did
in private at the breakfast table or the tea table or at
cocktail time. But never socially. Because I've always
had a theory: when you're out with friends, out
socially, everything must be charming, and you don't
allow the ugly.

"We don't even discuss the Negro question. Let's
forget they're only one-tenth of this country, and
what they're putting on, this act—someday they're
going to be stepped on like vermin. There's too much.
I'm starting a thing: equal rights for whites. I think
they've allowed themselves, with their necklaces and
their long hair and nonsense, to go too far.

"Now I've had the same manservant, who's Negro,
for thirty-three years, which is quite a record. I
suppose he's my closest friend in the world. He's a
great guy, Joseph."

STUDS TERKEL: "But aren't beads and necklaces worn by some of the
beautiful people today, too?"

SOCIALITE: "I was thinking tonight . . . I have to go out to
dinner, but I don't have my Malta Cross, which had
blue enamel and diamonds, which is really very good.
Because I loaned it to somebody. I'll have to wear what
I really love, which is my Zuñi Indian. This is authentic
and good, and people all accept that."[3]

DISC JOCKEY: "Do you mean to tell me, Professor, that you worked for
this car dealer for three months, and during this period,
you cheated hundreds of people by lying, stealing, and
manipulating?"

PROFESSOR: "Yes."

AUTHOR JOSEPH GELMIS:
"That sounds like chaos."

NORMAN MAILER: "That's the way I make films. If there isn't chaos in the making of it, then you can't get anything because everybody gets uptight. Because there's no script you've almost got to have a sort of chaos. It's the only way to get people relaxed enough so you can get something out of them."[4]

The Silent Put-on

A time comes in every put-on artist's life when he confronts a person who deserves the most sinister of all put-ons—the silent put-on. While downing cocktails, the middle-aged trucking executive begins to lecture you about how to throw a football pass. You, the perfect listener, nod vigorously, ask occasional and vague questions, and look attentive, while he straddles the nonexistent strings on the martini glass. Subtly and quite gradually, he begins to suspect, with or without reason, that you know a helluva lot more about football than he does. In fact, you probably are Roman Gabriel or Fran Tarkenton. When you begin looking at him with an expression of fantastic awe, he thinks he might've been gulled.

```
"(How in the hell do I get out of this?  God, I've
made a stupid ass of myself.)  Shirley--there's
Shirley--excuse me, I must run."
```

Of course, he never learns whether you are a football star, but in his mind he fantasizes some terrible visions. The most vicious of the genre, the silent put-on should be reserved for only the mighty, the cruel, or a relative.

The Close-Range or Conversational Put-on

The most obvious situation in which to use the put-on arises when you are pressed by a sympathetic but boorish questioner. It would be gauche to say, "Go to hell," or to dismiss him with a crude gesture; this kind of treatment is reserved for true enemies—Nazi or Cong. But what of the white liberal who wants to help the black? The liberal family man who wants to understand the homosexual? The father who wants to understand his wayward, dope-pushing youngster? The answer is the put-on, which is so

Chicago Sun-Times   Thursday, August 6, 1970

PEPITONE LEADS CUBS IN HUMOR

Sun-Times Correspondent

MONTREAL—Joe Pepitone hasn't made much of a splash in his six games with the Cubs and is batting only .222. But he is hitting 1,000 in the good humor league and, if nothing else, has brought a few laughs to the somber-faced Cubs.

Tuesday night when the Cubs were checking in for a three-game series with the Montreal Expos, there was the usual baggage delay because of customs; and the Cub party had to wait more than a half hour for the luggage to clear.

When the bags started coming through the shoot, dumping them to the bottom of a circular conveyor, the players pressed forward to claim their bags. The crowd was so thick and the conveyor so speedy that many players couldn't grab their bags out the first time around.

Pepitone, in the thick of this scene, acted as if he were an angry woman. Pursing his lips, he repeatedly pouted, "Oh, I wish somebody would find my purse. I've lost my purse."

Then, after a round or two later, Pepitone shouted to a Cub teammate who was at the other end of the conveyor, "Oh, would you please get that bag for me? My hairnets are in that bag."

As he mimicked powdering his nose, he lamented, "I've lost my hairpieces. What will I do?"

From someone else, perhaps, such remarks wouldn't necessarily draw any laughs. But Pepitone does, of course, carry several hairpieces with him.

---

elusive that the victim never knows what is happening. If the victim chooses to notice the put-on, the arranger can pretend innocence. It is a sure way to handle nuisances.

According to Brackman, there are two variations in conversational put-ons:

1. "Relentless agreement"—The arranger beats his victim to every cliché.
2. "Actualization of stereotype"—The arranger fulfills his victim's expectations.

In the "relentless" treatment, the arranger becomes the epitome of every negative expectation of the adversary. Example: A spinsterish brunette with her hair in a tight bun and her mouth in a tight smile encounters an alleged playboy at a cocktail party. She asks quite indirectly of the playboy's prowess. The supposed seducer responds:

```
"Sure, I look enormous and masculine, but it's all
a front.  When I get a female in bed, I can't
consummate the arrangement.  I guess I'm aggressive
with women to cover up my basic insecurities from
childhood."
```

In the "actualization" form, the playboy, if sadistic, can respond:

```
"Listen, honey, let's blow this joint (grabbing her
waist). We can go to my pad and then hit the sack.
What the hell, you'll love it with my gorgeous bod."
(Growling, nipping, and pawing, he yanks her toward
the exit.)
```

In either the "relentless" or "actualization" forms of the close-range put-on, the emphasis is upon fulfilling the questioner's preconceived notions. This goal requires the put-on artist to use broad, stereotyping gestures, as when the alleged playboy grabbed the woman's waist and used the clichés *pad* and *bod*. The black put-on artist may mimic a prizefighter's stance and praise Joe Louis, while the homosexual's put-on may include his batting his eyelashes and lamenting his perverted mother.

In any variation, the conversational put-on strategies make it impossible for someone not a part of an ingroup to become a member. It also reconfirms both parties' suspicions that communication has broken down and is not about to be reestablished.

The Interview/Conversational Put-on

Sometimes the encounter calls for a combination of different put-on techniques to achieve the desired results. This amalgam put-on strategy combines the ridicule of the questioner, as used in the interview put-on, with the ingratiation of the conversational put-on. At social gatherings it is an effective response to the incessant questions as to what you do for a living. If you are famous, powerful, or a snob, this put-on is an excellent choice.

"Hi, I'm Charlie Jones."
"Oh, I'm Winthrop Earl."
"What do you do, Winthrop?"
"I'm in the coat hanger business."
"The hanger business? Is there money in coat hangers?"
"Money? Millions. I've made millions. Got a plant in my basement, where I turn 'em out by the barrel . . . wife, kids—they all help."
"Is it complicated?"
"Complicated? There are 232 separate manufacturing operations to make one little wire hanger. To make a wooden hanger, there are—"
"Shirley! There's Shirley. Excuse me. I must run."

The Interview/Silent Put-on

As an innovative variation, this particular combination enables the person questioned to avoid the interview process altogether. The interview/ conversation put-on requires wit and audacity, while this combination requires only the latter. Upon being introduced, the put-on artist simply closes his eyes, starts blubbering, or begins a kind of deathlike gutteral croaking:

"Hi. I'm Charlie Jones." (A series of animal grunts . . . then a long, awkward pause.) "Shirley! There's Shirley. Excuse me. I must run."

The Put-on as Cop-out

The put-on is often used to cop out on a question. When an artist, teacher, or novelist is hard pressed to discover a solution for a problem or an embarrassing question, he can cop out. The style of his nonsolution, if couched as a put-on, frequently leaves the pursuer with an empty, mystified feeling. Example:

FILM CRITIC: "Mr. Smith, why do you take second-rate movie parts?"
SMITH: "Everyone's got a thing. Some people like pizza, others masturbation. I like playing in second-rate movies."
               (He smiles.)

Mr. Smith may not really know the answer to the question. Yet, the response, presented in self-mockery, saves him embarrassment. Even if he is aware that he is slipping and on the way down, the response still serves its purpose.

FAN: *(To drama critic, after the play.)* "How did you like the play?"
CRITIC: "It gave me a twinkle."

SPORTSCASTER: "Who are the greatest football players in history?"
SPORTS EXPERT: "Notre Dame, Southern Cal, and Parsons College."

As a mode of conduct, the cop-out has some serious drawbacks. The put-on artist who cops out may feel serene as he walks away from the encounter, only to have seriously damaged his possibilities for future communication. The defensiveness and insincerity of the cop-out, as with much of put-on behavior, leaves a victim with a certain amount of distrust for the perpetrator. When the put-on artist is hard pressed and serious about an issue, the former victim may not be able to distinguish this behavior from the put-on. This weakness makes the cop-out a treacherous weapon for self-presentation.

Despite the drawbacks and risks involved in using these verbal strategies, this has become the age of the put-on genius. The put-on has developed into a new mode of communication which pervades art, music, fashion, and even politics. Put-ons are so pervasive that an honest response frequently is cast into doubt. If Volkswagen manufacturers can put you on, can Durwood Kirby be far behind? "It costs a little more, but you use less." But the put-on has a certain charm, as do most of the other verbal games. It keeps the pompous ever vigilant, throws big brother off balance, and keeps headline writers well stocked with explosive banners:

POOR GET TAX BREAK

LAOS INVADED

BLAST DIMS MANHATTAN

QUESTIONS: THE PUT-ON

1. Billy Graham is a put-on.   T   F
2. Joe Namath is (circle one of the following):   kidder   pervert   put-on   quarterback   C. C. Rider   lisper
3. *Essay question.* Analyze this situation: Jim Zubin, a heavyweight boxer during the thirties, spied a famous sportswriter in a steam bath. Jim, quite fat now, grabbed the sportswriter and shouted, "I 'threw' every fight I ever fought. I could have been champ if I'd put out." "Why didn't you?" asked the sportswriter. "I needed the money," answered Jim.
4. Circle the correct number in the following statement: "In the famous experiment, the chicken pecked   10   15   25   40   times."

ANSWERS: THE PUT-ON

1. T and F.
2. None of the above.
3. An "A" answer will dwell on the symbolic significance of the word *spied*.
4. The psychologist who has been conducting this experiment since 1952 claims he has the chicken up to 845 pecks.

2 The Strategy of Redefinition

The strategy of redefinition was initially developed, in large part, by staff strategists in advertising agencies saddled with promoting a product carrying an undesirable image. Whether the merchandise is soap, deodorant, or automobiles, it has a product image; and if the image is negative, the product must be redefined and given a *new* image.

A striking example of product redefinition is the Dodge automobile. In the early fifties, researchers found that Dodge purchasers were largely old folk who thought the car appropriately dependable and sturdy. Unfortunately, upwardly mobile young Americans considered the Dodge stodgy, slow, and badly designed. They bought Chevrolets, Oldsmobiles, and Mercurys. The Dodge people, therefore, designed a new car with a larger "red ram" engine, and went after the young people with advertising that emphasized sleekness of design and boldness of performance. Because the new product was no longer sturdy and its performance was erratic, the Dodge lost not only the old folk, but it also failed to sell to the young. Not until fully ten years later, with introduction of the Charger and Super Bee series, did the car "catch on." Buttressed with tremendous success on the stock-car circuit, the new series this time made the redefinition believable.

An even more dramatic example of redefinition has been the successful campaign of blacks, both nonviolent and militant, to change the image of the lazy Negro. The stereotype many white Americans carried was that of the shuffling, indolent Negro who did absolutely nothing to emerge from self-imposed poverty. The image was indelibly stamped upon the black male by such film and radio personalities as Stepin Fetchit and Rochester—men seemingly cast forever in comic roles that characterized them as lacking in ambition, easily rattled, and invariably ordered about by whites:

"I'll watch'em, Boss." "Yassuh, Boss."

Not only were blacks determined to shatter this rigid, stultifying mold; they also decided to develop a novel cluster of identifying concepts with which to build a new image, employing such adjectival notions as "militant," "aggressive," and "black is beautiful." They thus began to alter the language structure itself. Suddenly the whites found themselves caught in a quandary of definition:

COLORED?   NEGRO?   BLACK?   AFRO-AMERICAN?

"I'm sure many of your Negro . . . I mean black friends will support the new curriculum. Ne . . . ah . . . Blacks will be empowered to run the Black Stud . . . ah . . . Afro-American Program."

"I don't mean anything derogatory by colored."

"Some of my best friends are ———."

Arthur L. Smith suggests that the vast significance of the redefinition process is in the blacks' restructuring of reality "with black men at the center." To accomplish this, as Smith points out, they employ a "reverse rhetoric":

Whereas most anthropological and sociological works by white authors describe the black man in comparison to the white man, the black revolutionists reverse the process. Their rhetoric suggests that, compared to the black man, the average white man exhibits the following physical traits: head slightly less elegant, nose less well developed, lips not so full, and hair stringy. The intent of this rhetoric is to get on the offensive by defining one's world in relationship to one's self, as indeed, the black revolutionists insist the white man has done for five hundred years.[3]

As Humpty Dumpty expressed it, "The question is . . . which is to be master—that's all."

Many other groups have adopted redefinition as a central strategy. The Gay Liberation movement has worked to alter the popular image of the homosexual. The stereotype of the limp-wristed, timid, terribly secretive homosexual is rooted in our culture. Parents frequently experience great anxiety if a son prefers dolls to football. The homosexual has worked underground because notice would bring public ridicule and possible unemployment. Leaders of the Gay Liberation movement altered their image of secrecy when they started sending to newspapers signed notices announcing that their meetings were open to the public. When a tavern in New York City allegedly discriminated against homosexuals, the Gay Libs became militant, first picketing and then smashing the bar—hardly timid behavior.

What groups in your community have successfully redefined themselves? What groups have failed?

Other examples of groups who have redefined themselves are the Women's Liberation Front, the American Indians, and the Chicanos. In each case, the group has suffered discrimination in economic, educational, and social opportunities. In each case, a more dominant group has imposed clusters of denigrating, image-negating adjectives. Each of these groups, as well as numerous others, has become militant and energetic in its attitude toward discriminative agencies and aggressive in its relationships with the media.

HELLO, I'M A CUTE AND FAIRLY TYPICAL CARTOON CHARACTER, AND I'LL BET THAT YOU THINK THAT I EXIST. OR MAYBE YOU DON'T. BUT EVEN IF YOU DON'T THINK I EXIST, I'M GOING TO SHOW YOU HOW I AM ABLE TO MANIPULATE YOU!

WELL, YOU JUST COME CLOSER AND WE'LL DECIDE WHETHER OR NOT I EXIST.

NOW, IF YOU LOOK CLOSE, WHAT DO YOU SEE?

THAT'S RIGHT! A LINE! NOT A LINE SEPARATING A SOLID OBJECT FROM THIN AIR, BUT JUST A LINE ON A PIECE OF PAPER. NOW, DON'T YOU FEEL SILLY LISTENING TO A LINE?

IF IT MAKES YOU FEEL ANY BETTER, JUST REMEMBER THAT A PEN LINE IS COMPOSED OF PARTICLES, JUST AS YOU ARE. BUT BY COGITO ERGO SUM, I ALSO EXIST, BECAUSE I THINK, OR RATHER, YOU THINK I THINK; THEREFORE, YOU MAKE ME EXIST.

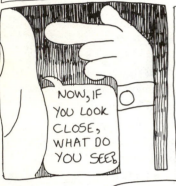

O.K. LET'S GET DOWN TO BUSINESS. FIRST YOU'LL NOTE THAT I AM FLOATING IN MIDAIR. THIS PROBABLY DOES NOT SURPRISE YOU BECAUSE BY THIS TIME YOU ARE USED TO SEEING CARTOON CHARACTERS DO STRANGE THINGS.

WE ALL KNOW THAT IT IS POSSIBLE FOR US CARTOON CHARACTERS TO DO ANYTHING AT ALL. FOR INSTANCE, I CAN SEPARATE MY HEAD FROM MY NECK AND AT THE SAME TIME CONTINUE TO TALK. AS AN ADDED BONUS, I'LL STRETCH MY ARM INTO A DOUGHNUT...

BUT THERE IS SOMETHING THAT I COULD DO THAT MIGHT SHOCK YOU. WATCH CAREFULLY AS I RESHAPE MY LINES.

WHAT I HAVE JUST DONE IS TO SHIFT MY STYLE FROM CUTE CARTOON TO SCIENCE-FICTION SEMI-REALISM. THE REASON FOR YOUR PROBABLE SURPRISE IS THAT YOU HAVE BEEN FORCED TO QUICKLY REDEFINE YOUR VIEWS.

WE'LL GET BACK TO REDEFINITION OF VIEWS IN A MOMENT, BUT FIRST YOU'RE PROBABLY WONDERING WHY A FLOATING ONOMATOPOEIA IS TALKING TO YOU INSTEAD OF THE SILVERY DUDE ON THE OTHER PAGE.

WELL, IF YOU LOOK CAREFULLY AT THE PRECEDING PAGE, YOU WILL SEE THAT THE LAST WORD BALLOON IS POINTING AT THE DOT OF THE FIRST EXCLAMATION POINT. THIS MIGHT AT FIRST INDICATE THAT IT IS THE DOT SPEAKING. BUT IN THE FIRST PANEL ON THIS PAGE YOU SEE THE SECOND DOT SPEAKING.

BECAUSE OF CONTINUITY OF DIALOGUE YOU TEND NOT TO BELIEVE THAT THE TWO DOTS ARE SPEAKING INDEPENDENTLY OF EACH OTHER; SO, BECAUSE OF THE PRESENCE OF A LARGER WHOLE OF WHICH THE DOTS ARE PARTS, YOU ARE LEFT BELIEVING THAT IT IS THE LARGER WHOLE SPEAKING.

BUT I'VE FOOLED YOU AGAIN! I'VE ACTUALLY BEEN THROWING MY VOICE AND HIDING BEHIND THIS PANEL ALL ALONG!

WORD BALLOONS ARE VERY IMPORTANT MANIPULATORS.

BY THE PRINCIPLE ABOVE, YOU WERE LED TO BELIEVE THAT THE METALLIC FIGURE WAS SPEAKING—BECAUSE HE WAS PART OF A LARGER WHOLE AND A MORE LOGICAL SPEAKER. JUST AS THE WORD "ZAM" WAS MORE LIKELY TO BE SPEAKING INSTEAD OF THE DOTS, SO WAS THE HUMANOID FIGURE MORE LIKELY TO TALK. WORD BALLOONS ARE EXTREMELY IMPORTANT, BECAUSE IN CARTOONS THERE ARE NO MOVING LIPS AND NO AUDIBLE LINKS TO BE MADE.

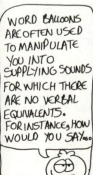

WORD BALLOONS ARE OFTEN USED TO MANIPULATE YOU INTO SUPPLYING SOUNDS FOR WHICH THERE ARE NO VERBAL EQUIVALENTS. FOR INSTANCE, HOW WOULD YOU SAY...

OR, IF YOU WERE EGYPTIAN WOULD YOU TALK LIKE THIS...

NOW, BACK ON PAGE ONE WE WERE TALKING ABOUT REDEFINITION. LET'S GET ON WITH IT!

THE MOST COMMON USE OF REDEFINITION IN THE COMICS TODAY IS PROBABLY THE UNDERGROUND COMICS.

COSMIC POOPOO FUNNIES

FOR EXAMPLE, IF THIS WAS AN UNDERGROUND COMIC, I WOULD PROBABLY BE A SICKENINGLY CUTE BUNNY RABBIT, OR SOMETHING SIMILAR.

YOUR EXPECTATIONS ARE GEARED SO THAT YOU EXPECT ME TO DO CUTE BUNNY-LIKE THINGS AND BE, IN GENERAL, A NICE, LOVABLE LITTLE CREATURE.

BUT, IF I WERE OOF GRUNT TO SUDDENLY AND GRAPHICALLY MOLEST AND SIMULTANEOUSLY KNIFE A TWELVE-YEAR-OLD, YOU WOULD BE FORCED TO REDEFINE YOUR CONCEPTS DRASTICALLY AND QUICKLY, RESULTING IN SOME AMOUNT OF SHOCK FOR YOU.

THIS IS, OF COURSE, QUITE INTENTIONAL AND OCCASIONALLY DOWNRIGHT NAUSEATING. BUT THIS USE OF MANIPULATION IS A STRATEGY USED TO MAKE THE READER MORE AWARE OF HIS OWN CONCEPTS. THIS STRATEGY IS VERY SIMILAR TO THE PUT-ON.

ASIDE FROM THE UNDERGROUND STRIPS, GENERALLY SPEAKING, THE PURPOSE OF THE COMICS IS TO ENTERTAIN AND THEREBY MAKE MONEY FOR THE PUBLISHER.

THE WAY THIS HAS BEEN ACCOMPLISHED IN THE PAST HAS REQUIRED LITTLE WORK ON THE PART OF THE ARTIST-WRITER. HE HAS HAD TO USE THE COMIC STRIP FORM TO ITS MINIMAL POTENTIAL AND SIMPLY MANIPULATE THE AUDIENCE INTO BELIEVING THAT ANYTHING CAN HAPPEN IN A COMIC STRIP. THE IMPOSSIBLE MADE POSSIBLE, OR AT LEAST PLAUSIBLE, HAS ALWAYS BEEN ENTERTAINING AND ALWAYS WILL BE.

SPIDER MAN

BUT AS OF LATE, COMIC-BOOK PRODUCERS HAVE FOUND THAT IT IS IMPORTANT TO MANIPULATE THE AUDIENCE INTO BELIEVING THAT THEIR SUPER-HERO CHARACTERS ARE HUMAN BEINGS, JUST LIKE YOU AND ME... MAKING THE WORLD OF FANTASY THAT MUCH CLOSER THROUGH IDENTIFICATION.

AND MOSES SAID UNTO THEM, "BANANAS!"

I'LL EXPLAIN THAT PANEL IN A MINUTE. BUT FIRST LET ME EXPLAIN THAT I'VE JUST KILLED OFF THE LITTLE NARRATOR AND HE WON'T BE BACK.

YOU SEE, I'VE BEEN MANIPULATING YOU ALL ALONG. I'VE TRIED TO CREATE A LOVABLE LITTLE CHARACTER, EASY TO RELATE TO. RARELY IS SUCH A CHARACTER KILLED IN A COMIC STRIP BECAUSE IF YOU HAD BEEN IDENTIFYING WITH THAT CHARACTER, YOU PROBABLY WOULD STOP BUYING THAT STRIP. NOW, ABOUT THAT PANEL. I JUST WANTED TO DEMONSTRATE...

HOW CINEMATIC THE COMIC STRIP FORM IS, AND HOW, BY INSERTING AN INCONGRUOUS ELEMENT INTO THE FLOW, A READER CAN BE SHOCKED. IN STRUCTURE, THE COMIC STRIP CAN BE PICTORAL NARRATIVE AND NOT NECESSARILY CINEMATIC. THE COMIC STRIP CAN NEVER HOPE TO COMPETE WITH FILM IN TERMS OF MANIPULATION, BUT CAN, HOWEVER, THROUGH VISUAL APPEAL, HUMOR, AND THE STRATEGIES OF MANIPULATION DISCUSSED EARLIER, PROVE ITSELF TO BE A STRONG DEVICE FOR MANIPULATION.

Redefinition and Behavioral Change

An axiom of redefinition strategy is that *behavior* change must accompany the verbal assertions of an image change. Eventually the group striving for redefinition must adjust its life style and actions to reinforce the new language—the new adjectival clusters—thereby consummating the strategy. The Dodge division, for example, successfully achieved the redefinition of its bold, new image only when the company produced a bold, new, reliable car. The riots in Watts, Detroit, and Newark went a long way in consummating the image change for blacks. The same can be said for the Gay Libs' smashing of bars, the Women's Libs' confrontation with *Playboy*'s Hugh Hefner, the American Indians' occupation of Alcatraz Island, and the Chicanos' victory in the Delano fruit strike. These instances clearly evidence that the principle of redefinition, to be effective, must go beyond the verbal stage and into the *action* stage—that the strategists who employ it must somehow "lay themselves" on the line.

However, a number of problems complicate the relationship between verbal redefinition and behavior change. One of these is the danger of over-selling the image so that further modification is impossible. Members of the Chicago street gang, the Black P. Stone Nation, which controls much of the city's sprawling South Side urban ghetto, early defined themselves as anticop, insolent, and enormously gifted in maneuvering amidst the alleys and subways of Chicago. In the mid-sixties, however, both police and public pressure began to hamper their burgeoning extortion activities. Seemingly, the Stones sensed a need to alter their public image, and one possible solution was to legitimatize their activities and thereby stymie harrassment.

During this period the organization changed its name from the Blackstone Rangers to the Black P. Stone Nation, which encompassed their growing conglomerate of gangs and afforded them a less militant identification. The Nation's leader, Jeff Fort, began calling press conferences to express the organization's view toward ghetto problems and to announce public service programs such as free breakfasts for school children and back-to-school parades. In addition, a number of government and public grants were made available to the Stones to help them implement a variety of community-controlled programs.

However, the Stones have never been successful in redefining their image. Members of the organization frequently have undercut the redefinition with purported murders and strong-arm tactics. They have continued to erode community support by intimidating black school children in middle-class neighborhoods. They are suspected of funneling grant money into illegal operations. And, finally, responsible black leaders have criticized or denounced them openly. For example, the Reverend Jesse Jackson, as head of Operation Breadbasket, labeled the Nation a menace to the black people. The Stones' drive for redefinition appears to be failing, as do the efforts of such other black groups as the Black Panthers and the Conservative Vice Lords.

The Stones failed, in large part, because they did not control the negative image-makers within their own group. There always were individual members of the organization who, in need of some quick money, soloed in a mugging or shook down a neighborhood grocer without authorization. To be successful, redefinition requires tight organizational control and discipline. In organization terminology, it means divesting your group of deadwood.

How did the Marlboro cigarette commercials redefine the company image? What other companies have drastically redefined their product's image?

Redefinition: Controlling Agents

One of the most important tasks of redefinition is to determine who is to do the defining and who (or what) is to be defined. In many instances, the definer is not the person being defined. Consider these examples:

1. A father decides that he wants his son to be a dentist; and to this end, he rewards him for high grades in science, sends him away to a prep school, and bankrolls him through dental school. Part of growing up is doing your own defining.

Who controls your image?

2. A liberal professor finds himself identified with the conservative wing of the faculty group on campus. This paradox has occurred because, during a university confrontation, he has sided with one of two moderate groups formed to negotiate issues. Group 1 (the one

with which the professor was not associated) quickly took a middle-of-the-road position, thereby forcing Group 2 to make a choice between moving further left of center or further to the right. The latter group went slightly right and were promptly labeled conservative. Here, Group 1 was the definer: it redefined the liberal faculty member, sticking him with a label which he did not want and which he probably did not deserve.

The Role of the Media in Redefinition

In any society dominated by mass communication, any one of the media—or any combination of them—must be recognized as a powerful redefiner. An interesting example of this principle could be seen in the television series, "The Courtship of Eddie's Father." Here we see a subtle but distinct redefinition of the elements that supposedly constitute a happy American family. Previously, any family with a widowed or divorced parent generally had been considered a public disaster of sorts. In this series, however, the situation was reconstructed. A widowed but happy father kept his young son entertained and content in a high-rise apartment building. The father, though he periodically lamented the loss of his late wife, had an abundance of lovely, attentive female companions who also lavished attention on the young son. The program attempted to redefine for American audiences what constitutes a happy, wholesome, well-adjusted family existence. In fact, Eddie's situation seemed considerably more appealing and enjoyable than that of most other children.

The comic books are another example of the media's influence on redefinition. When their hero suddenly turned modern, Superman's fans became aware of the mass media's power to redefine. Millions of comic-book lovers knew the story of Clark Kent, the stodgy, mild-mannered newspaper reporter for the *Metropolis Daily Planet* who monthly transformed himself into a man of steel. It was a rude jolt to find that the capricious publisher had redefined Clark as a swinging, network TV reporter for the Galaxy Broadcasting System. Although fans were grateful when the publisher gave Lois Lane a face-lifting, the shock of a wide-tied, contemporary Clark Kent stunned many readers. After all, no one had asked the public if they wanted Clark updated. But there he was, redefined. The only solace for a grieving comic-book readership was to redefine themselves as fans of the new Superman or to cop out and buy Plastic Man.

In actual practice, not only does a given medium serve powerfully as a redefiner, but also the exercise of this power rests very largely with the medium's editor. Whether he directs the choice of the newspaper stories to be given prominence or is the television editor who snips fifteen minutes of

TV film time down to thirty seconds, *he* is the ultimate definer. Usually it is the editor who decides if California's Chicano leader-organizer, Cesar Chavez, is to be featured in *Esquire*, if he is to appear on a television network's six-o'clock news slot, or if his activities on behalf of the grape pickers are to be reported on page 1 or page 41 of the morning's newspaper. To be sure, such other factors as timeliness and comparative importance sometimes heavily influence story choice and placement in the media, but beyond these situational dictates, much of the option-taking rests with the editor.

In view of television's vast range and potency, the fact that it actually selects and redefines the leadership of various movements should come as no surprise. In the Berkeley Free Speech movement, for instance, television crews and lensmen found Mario Savio so photogenic and colorful that they focused on him and rarely publicized the true leadership. Similarly, at Columbia University, Mark Rudd—because of his provocative speech-making— was singled out as the leader and given extensive exposure on TV screens everywhere. By defining or redefining leadership of movements in this way, television networks can manipulate to a large extent the outcome of a protest.

Redefinition and Political Transformation

Television's immense capability for redefinition was unquestionably a powerful factor in the come-back miracle of President Nixon. If ever a public figure needed redefining, it was Richard Milhous Nixon. Originally, the medium's cameras had caught him in some of the most uncomplimentary situations in American political history. Here was Nixon debating John F. Kennedy and looking like a blackjawed enforcer for the Mafia, or like a high-pressure used-car salesman with a five-o'clock shadow. Later, here was Nixon again appearing on television after losing the California governorship and bitterly blaming the media. To many Americans, the public image of Nixon was that of a petty, vindictive loser.

The approach of the 1968 presidential campaign created a need for a new image. The solution? Go back onto the TV screens and be redefined as a solid, cool winner. Nixon's campaign strategists were not reluctant to discuss the techniques of transforming the man.

```
. . . to present Nixon the Man in ways that will
dispel existing negative feelings about his person-
ality and sincerity--that will show him as a knowl-
edgeable, experienced, and likeable candidate.  Our
efforts in the primaries proved this to be an
attainable objective.
                --Harry Treleaven, advertising manager[4]
```

People are stirred by the legend, including the living legend, not by the man himself. It's the aura
that surrounds the charismatic figure more than it
is the figure itself that draws the followers. Our
task is to build the aura.
                    --William Gavin, speechwriter[5]

Standing adds to his "feel of confidence" and the
viewers' "feel" of his confidence.
   The "arena" effect is excellent, and he plays to
all areas well. The look has "guts."
   Generally, he has a very "Presidential" look and
style--he smiles easily (and looks good doing it).
He should continue to make lighter comments once in
a while for pacing.
                       --Roger Ailes, producer[6]

. . . there would not have to be a "new Nixon."
Simply a new approach to television.
                    --Raymond K. Price, speechwriter[7]

The Strategy of Redefinition: Some Disadvantages— and Advantages

If we examine the strategy of redefinition critically, one drawback will soon
become apparent: the process—especially if we are doing the defining—
usually occurs at the expense of someone else. This, in fact, appears nearly
inescapable. Almost any group will quickly find that it must compare
itself with some other group—and that, more often than not, such comparison
must be odious. A frequent target for odious comparison are WASPs, who
presumably control much of America. (For a further note on WASPs, see
Chapter 3, "Stereotyping and Minorities.") Or, further, consider that the
Women's Lib *must* define men negatively, the Gay Lib feels *compelled* to
downgrade heterosexuals, and teachers' unions feel *obliged* to assail
administrators. This, admittedly, is at the very least a divisive tactic—and it
can be a highly destructive one. Attempts have been made to explain or
excuse this human tendency to make the competition look bad. *The spirit
of competition* has been used as a blanket euphemism. Groups on the rise,
it may be, need a scapegoat. Or, perhaps, nature simply abhors a vacuum.
Whatever the explanation, it would seem that—as a variant of Newton's
Law—"For everything or everybody that goes up, something or somebody
else has to come down."

Among the advantages of the strategy of redefinition, we can point out that once the new image is implanted, members will begin modeling themselves along the lines of the new definition, the new adjectival clusters: black children become proud, even militant; women assume corporation presidencies; public school teachers strike for smaller classes. It would not be difficult to deduce a national mania for redefinition.

Redefinition is certainly not new; as an ongoing and ever-present process energizing most human relationships, it has been with us for several thousand years. What *is* new in this Electronic Age is the speed with which the media redefine individuals and groups. Fortunately, as a saving grace, redefinition can occur only as fast as information can be disseminated, only as rapidly as the public mind can be bombarded with adjectival clusters and implications. When redefinition can be accomplished by taking a pill or drinking a potion, we might start looking for another concept.

3 Stereotyping and Minorities

Historically, stereotyping has been used to humble society's most truculent underdogs. Typically, this strategy finds the oppressing majority describing the minority in broadly inclusive, denigrative categories. The nonliberated, white, Protestant suburbanite calls Jews "Hebes," "kikes," or the more subtly refined "aggressive." If the White, Anglo-Saxon Protestant (WASP) becomes irritated with the black conductor on his commuter train, he may call him "nigger," "lazy," or the more refined "underprivileged." What especially distinguishes this strategy is that it compels the underdog to defend himself on the ground dictated by the stereotyper; that is, he must defend himself on the stereotyper's terms: "I'm *not* cheap," or "I *don't* steal." As long as WASPs could stereotype their victims and receive in return only a defensive, nonthreatening response, the strategy satisfied them.

Is the term WASP a stereotype?

The WASPs were willing even to surrender the moral advantage to the oppressed, allowing them the dubious satisfaction of protesting their innocence in morally outraged tones: "They're out to get me," "They're unfair," "Why don't those bastards leave me alone?" The oppressed groups could also use the stereotyping slurs as rallying cries to try to build protective organizations and to support ethnic movements. Where would the B'nai B'rith, Sons of Italy, or the Knights of Columbus be today without the threat of the WASP?

Now, however, the situation may be turning around. The moral advantage seems no longer to be wholly with the minority; it may even be wafting WASPward. This paradox is attributable in part to the fact that, with their tighter organization and easy access to the media, minority groups are now themselves stereotyping with a ferocity unparalleled in American history. Consider this example:

Slave-catchers, slaveowners, murderers, butchers, invaders, oppressors—the white heroes have acquired new names. The great white statesmen whom school children are taught to revere are revealed as the architects of systems of human exploitation and slavery.

--Eldridge Cleaver[1]

It is beginning to be apparent, in any case, that WASPs no longer have a monopoly on stereotyping as a tactic. Indeed, with increasing frequency they are becoming the victims more often than the perpetrators. The WASP is now the object of much strategic manipulation. It is his daughter whom blacks, Mexicans, Jews, Indians, and Poles are eager to ravish. It is his split-level-housed neighborhood that the NAACP (National Association for the Advancement of Colored People) wants to integrate. His are the values that men's and women's liberation movements desire to change. It is even the WASP's money that the government wants to use in order to put an end to poverty.

Conversation in Lake Forest

The Conversers:

HUSBAND,   *six feet two, steel-gray hair, with a Ford Country Wagon in the driveway.*

WIFE,   *blond, thin, well-dressed, the mother of three beautiful children.*

HUSBAND: They're striking my plant again.

WIFE: What do they want, Arthur?

HUSBAND: More jobs.

WIFE: More jobs?

HUSBAND: More jobs.

WIFE: I suppose they deserve it after all these years of . . .

HUSBAND: I worked hard to get where I am, Margaret!

WIFE: I know, Arthur. But they don't get executive positions. They're the janitors, the garbage men, the shoe . . .

HUSBAND: I was fired today.

WIFE: *(After a gasp.)* Dirty niggers.

HUSBAND: *(Nods.)* Dirty niggers . . .

WIFE:
HUSBAND: *(In unison.)* Dirty niggers.

Watch Your Language

Having lost his rhetorical advantage, the WASP has taken to a number of alternative strategies—strategies which previously were the domain of the very rich. Having been stereotyped as prejudiced, he combats the image by engaging in a number of "liberal" activities and by surrounding himself with symbols that indicate his *non*prejudice. He joins Operation Breadbasket, and puts on his front window a Breadbasket sign calling for open housing. (He knows he is safe, of course, because he is well aware that the suburb where he lives will not allow minorities.) Twice a year, he attends Breadbasket banquets where he laughs appreciatively at the jokes of Dick Gregory, meanwhile stoking up his moral righteousness. At cocktail parties, he and his wife counter any racial slur with the smug pronouncement: "We don't talk that way," or "I wish you wouldn't use that expression." They go home knowing that they are liberal and that all the bigots at the party know it. They know also that there is little risk in this strategy, since it is not fashionable to utter racial slurs publicly at WASP parties.

Can a non-WASP be a WASP?

Walk

There are other counterstrategies which WASPs can safely employ and which are equally viable. These include marching for peace or participating in the caravan of food. The latter is particularly rewarding. Twice yearly, the caravan gathers food from among the wealthy; and on a warm, sunny Sunday morning (a safe time), they drive in the caravan to the ghetto, where they distribute their goodies. These are a few of the advantages:

You can see first-hand what has happened to your old neighborhood.
You get your kids out of bed and out of the house.
You "one-up" other liberals by talking solemnly about your first-hand knowledge of conditions in the ghetto.

The march for peace or for open housing or for whatever can be equally strategic. Again, your kids will enjoy the walk, and the neighbors—knowing that the march is not a threat—will understand. If, unexpectedly, the "walk" turns violent, you can always pretend that you were merely out for a Sunday stroll.

Who feels for the WASP?
Paul Harvey, Spiro Agnew,
John Wayne, Rev. Carl McIntyre,
Colonel Ky, Lawrence Welk,
Niemann-Marcus, Jimmy Stewart
?

. . . And thus the stereotyper is stereotyped . . .

4 The Confrontation Strategy

In the past decade, the strategy of confrontation has been more than merely
influential. Confrontation, according to *Life* Magazine, "threatens the whole
tradition of democratic dialogue in America."[1] The message of those
dissidents who practice confrontation is unmistakable: "The System doesn't
listen. The only thing this country responds to is power." Disruption has
become an integral part of the American life style. The mass media, fascinated
by the drama inherent in the confrontation strategy, frequently escalate
the disruption to nationwide notice. Subsequent quelling by the National
Guard or repression by police quite often draws wide attention and sympathy
to the "movement," whatever it happens to be. During demonstrations over

Nixon's Cambodia invasion during the spring of 1970, the National Guard's killing of four students at Kent State triggered a chain of demonstrations and strikes in colleges and universities all across the country. The televised newscast of students' being gunned down turned dinner-table conversations to the horror of killing. As thousands of administrators, mayors, and wardens have discovered to their dismay—and ofttimes to their personal discomfort—confrontation is a potent weapon.

In the overall view, dissidents see the protest as a series of escalations producing, first, dramatic confrontation and, ultimately, genuinely beneficial communication. The protesters reason that, by suffering the pain and uncertainty of head-cracking, rides in paddy wagons, and all-night vigils, they will influence other people to get together to talk about poor housing, inadequate teaching, or poor wages. Sometimes this is the outcome; sometimes it is not. But the irony is that coercion in the form of a confrontation is apparently necessary to reinstitute the democratic process.

Productive confrontation is of course much more than a mere series of loosely energized or happenstance escalations. Every detail of the entire maneuver demands careful groundwork and intricate timing. Confrontations frequently entail large-scale, lengthy operations, and every phase must be planned logistically. In fact, what every college needs these days (and has hesitated to ask for until now) is a *Confrontation Manual* consisting of two parts: "Helpful Hints for Successful Confrontation" and "Timely Tips for the New-Style Administrator."

Helpful Hints for Successful Confrontation

In succinct sequence, Part One of the *Manual* would look something like this:

1. Plan carefully and shrewdly.
2. Select a simple issue that can be sloganized, shouted, and reshaped as necessary to include the complaints of new recruits to the cause.
3. Be seen—and obscene—as the linguistic and confrontational tactics and timing may dictate.
4. Constantly escalate your demands.
5. Finally and ultimately, CONFRONT—get busted.

If you follow all of these steps faithfully to their inevitable conclusion, your head may be bloody and slightly bowed, but your "cause" may emerge triumphant.

Admittedly, it's not easy to walk the lines just laid down. So let's take a second look at each of them in turn.

Plan the Entire Operation Carefully

A confrontation involving the take-over of a public building, a dean's office, or even the occupying of a hallway means blankets, grass, beer, cokes, sandwiches—the usual homey comforts.

The seemingly slight problem of sandwiches, for example, has vexed many a radical leader. How many to order? What kinds? Much depends on the age and ethnic background of the agitators, regardless of the cause for which they may be agitating. It would be equally foolish to order ham sandwiches for Brandeis University or caviar for an elementary school. Hardhats on strike, for instance, have been known to consume eleven sandwiches apiece during an all-night sit-in in Manhattan. The strike at Harvard University in 1969 was distinguished for its tasty fare, and it was prominently admired by the team of University students who wrote an account of the event:

```
The efforts of the food committee . . . won the
most plaudits.  Its members collected nearly $200
for supplies.  Beginning about 3:00, they began to
bring in large cartons containing food supplies of
all kinds, and such amenities as straws, paper plates,
and napkins. . . .  By 5:30, a huge stockpile had
been accumulated inside the occupied building.
When the meeting in the Faculty Room adjourned
after 6:00, the students lounged all over the build-
ing, eating bologna sandwiches and sipping orange
soda. . . . The tables of two large rooms on the
first floor were piled high with food.  Throughout
the evening, anyone who wanted something to eat could
merely walk in and help himself.²
```

From a great university like Harvard, of course, one would expect the best in revolution cuisine. In contrast, at one of the small junior colleges a strategical sit-in collapsed when the food committee could produce only uncolored oleo and Ritz crackers.

The individual or group planning a confrontation should observe certain other social and communicational amenities. A very important nicety is to be sure to call the media and inform them of the impending take-over, sit-in, march, or flag-burning. At the same time, make certain that you tell the radio, television, and newspaper people specifically *who* will be keeping them "officially" informed as the confrontation develops. If possible, provide them with a timetable and leave no doubt as to *where* and *when* the culminating phase of the event, the confrontation itself, will be taking place. The field media people have witnessed so many confrontations that they are not necessarily enthralled by the prospect of having to cover still another one. As a cameraman for the American Broadcasting Company was heard to complain during the 1970 strike at Northwestern University: "I hate these demonstrations—they're damn dangerous. I'd rather be in Vietnam." If you want the reporters to continue to write and the television crewmen to keep grinding away, the very least you can do is to extend them the courtesy of telling them where the action is, where it is heading, and at what time.

Select a Simple, Sloganizable Issue

To confront successfully, you must discover and succinctly define issues which are attractive to large numbers of students. Emotional or moral commitment is not essential—at least not in the beginning. However, emotional upheaval or moral outrage can be decisive assets, especially in matters of timing. At the start, the planners of the confrontation may *contrive* an issue, since the group's real position will emerge later when the student body has been sufficiently stirred and radicalized. This duplicity is not an unusual tactic among protest groups. For example, the Saul Alinsky organization in Chicago wanted a reordering of priorities in national policies; but after a door-to-door survey in the suburbs indicated a strong interest in pollution, the organization decided to begin by waging an *ecology* campaign.* The Alinsky strategy is to work back to the national-priorities issue after building a strong local organization on the basis of pollution. This type of reasoning has often characterized the selecting of the issues in building confrontations.

The demonstrations at Columbia University illustrate this strategem of first contriving an issue and then allowing the real ones to evolve from it. The *apparent* issue at Columbia was the impending construction of the Morningside Park Gymnasium, which was to border on Harlem. This, to the black radicals, seemed to symbolize the building of a "Berlin wall" between the University and the black communities. To this "gym-crow" issue was joined a demand that Columbia discontinue its affiliation with the Institute for Defense Analysis, a loose confederation of universities organized to offer advice to the Federal government in matters of defense, research on weapons and tactics, and riot control. The *real* issue was something else. And SDS (Students for a Democratic Society) activist Mark Rudd, speaking in Boston after the Columbia confrontation, admitted as much:

*Saul Alinsky is considered by many to be this country's foremost organizer of community-action groups.

Let me tell you, we manufactured those issues. The Institute for Defense Analysis is nothing at Columbia. Just three professors. And the gym issue is bull. It doesn't mean anything to anybody. I had never been to the gym site before April 23. I didn't even know how to get there.[3]

John R. Searle, in writing "A Foolproof Scenario for Student Revolts," explains how the transformation of issues from the contrived to the real plays an essential role in what he refers to as the creation of a rhetorical climate:

In Stage Two the original issue is transformed so that the structure of authority in the university is itself the target. This is achieved by the following method. The fact that the university rejected the original demands and, even more, the fact that the university disciplined people for rule violations in making those demands are offered as conclusive proof that the university is the real enemy of the forces of truth and justice on the Sacred Topic. Thus, if the original demand was related to the war in Viet Nam, the fact that the university disciplined a student for rule violation in making the demand is proof that the university is really working for the war and that it is out to "crush dissent." If, for example, the demonstrations were against Dow Chemical Company recruiters on campus, the fact of university discipline proves that the university is really the handmaiden (or whore) of the military-industrial complex. And the fact that the university refuses to cancel plans for the gym (Columbia) or does cancel plans for the Cleaver course (Berkeley) demonstrates that the university is really a racist institution. Why would anybody try to discipline our fellow students and refuse our just demands if they weren't racists, warmongers, or dissent-crushers, as the case may be? And, indeed, can't we now see that the university is really just a part of much larger forces of oppression (imperialism, racism) in our American society? In the face of such proof, only the most callous or evil would fail to join us in our struggle to make this a livable university, a place where we can truly be free.[4]

There is a certain degree of hazard in concealing the real issue or issues until some kind of coalition of support has been achieved. Certainly the tactic explains some of the more bizarre events that occur during confrontations. In the initial stage of the conflict, this issue-concealment is almost sure to produce disagreements among the many groups as they try to focus on the real, underlying demand or demands. Frequently, the participants will split into divergent groups because some of the demonstrators are fighting for the original issues (mostly moderates), while others (mostly militants) are operating on the real issue: *the structure of authority*—which runs to the very core of almost any institution whether it be educational, governmental, political, or religious.

Eventually, confrontation issues have to be translated into *words*. Issues have to be converted into slogans—short, succinct, shoutable slogans, slogans to be chanted and clearly understood, slogans to vivify and—not infrequently— to invoke violence. In sloganizing your issues, select words which lack precise definitions. Make sure the words are short and emotional, thereby suitable for group shouts. "Dean Smith is a misanthrope" isn't going to rally thousands to your cause.

Any list of successful slogans would be almost endless. Campuses, civic centers, parks, and streets have resounded to the chants of:

HELL, NO! WE WON'T GO!
CLOSE IT DOWN! CLOSE IT DOWN!
ROTC MUST GO!
I AM SOMEBODY! I AM SOMEBODY!
POWER TO THE PEOPLE!
OVERCOME! OVERCOME!

Assuming that you have planned well and that you have pinpointed the issues (both real and contrived) in an energetic, chantable slogan, you are now ready to move into the third phase.

Be Seen—and Obscene

Phases One and Two, as you have probably noted, are essentially initiatory tasks worked out privately. In Phase Three you move onto the "public" stage, to directly encounter your adversaries. This means becoming visible, and you will of course be much more "visible" if you are *vocal*. It's time to give vent to your excitement, anger, outrage, or contempt. This means refining—or coarsening—the language you have employed in evolving your slogans. And you also carry your linguistic efforts several steps further.

Don't hesitate to shout escalatory words, inflammatory words, words well calculated to anger, upset, even up-end the adversary. In confrontational linguistics, nothing is quite as nerve-shattering and reaction-producing as an obscene epithet, especially if it reflects unfavorably upon the political origins or the ancestral validity of your adversary. If you start out on a fairly modest plane and let yourself get carried away as the confrontation accelerates, you might include any number of these favorites:

FASCIST
RACIST
LIAR
TRAITOR
PIG
MOTHERFUCKER

The last, in particular, has been known to set off a wild melee of club-swinging and head-bleeding.

If you have any luck, your adversary will be maneuvered into making defensive public announcements such as "I'm sick of being called a fascist," which will only have the effect of implying to a bemused public that he is indeed a fascist. Further, the fact that the target of your invective will be obligated to answer your epithets will serve to encourage less vociferous supporters because most participants in a confrontation harbor a secret passion to see institutional authorities up against the wall.

Constantly Escalate Your Demands

Assuming that you have advanced through the foregoing phases with at least a modicum of success and not too much blood-letting, you may correctly suppose that your strategy is working. But even if the triumphs up to this point have been minimal, or if for some reason you have failed entirely, never admit it. If you have no real demands, invent a few. Somehow, appropriate a mimeograph machine and crank out more daily ultimatums. Every morning, when your opponent sits down to breakfast, he should discover a new demand. "Oh, God," he will mutter as he gulps his orange juice, "the Polish students want a Polish Student Union!"

This constant escalating of demands serves three useful purposes. First, it keeps the administration continuously off balance. Every time they seem to feel they have made the necessary compromises and concessions, they immediately find that you have added demands and redefined the situation. Second, escalation ridicules the orderly process of negotiation and compromise. Third, the strategy enables and encourages new supporting groups to add *their* demands.

What communication situations (if any) justify confrontation strategies?

You must be careful never to appear to have closed the door on the possible *negotiability* of your demands. Nor should you present such a lengthy list as to make their achievement impractical or seemingly impossible. James Forman, in his "Manifesto to White Christian Churches and Jewish Synagogues," stated it well: ". . . our demands are negotiable, but they cannot be minimized."[5] And then he proceeded to sloganize his group's objectives as being:

> ALL ROADS MUST LEAD TO REVOLUTION
> UNITE WITH WHOMEVER YOU CAN UNITE
> NEUTRALIZE WHEREVER POSSIBLE
> FIGHT OUR ENEMIES RELENTLESSLY
> VICTORY TO THE PEOPLE
> LIFE AND GOOD HEALTH TO MANKIND
> RESISTANCE TO DOMINATION BY WHITE CHRISTIAN CHURCHES
>   AND JEWISH SYNAGOGUES
> REVOLÚTIONARY BLACK POWER
> WE SHALL WIN WITHOUT A DOUBT

Confront Your Adversary

There comes a time in every confrontation when somebody—you or your opponent—must resort to physical action. As the "activist," *you* should be the controlling agent; you—and not your adversary—must be in a position to make all of the essential choices. *You* select the form of the action to be taken: marches, strikes, sit-ins, occupation of buildings, barricades. Make the "pigs" come after you. A People's Park is an excellent site on which to gather your forces. For some reason, the city authorities object when a playground is dug up or a street barricaded in order to provide a liberated zone. The police will storm in to evacuate you from the area.

Try to maneuver the police into removing you from the premises. If they are recalcitrant, be as rude and aggressive as possible. If the police come in, there is bound to be some kind of brutality, by the nature of the removal business. The head-splitting will bring in moderate students who are generally incensed by seeing fellow students maimed. (*Note:* When the bust is imminent, be somewhere else. It hurts to be busted and you won't want to miss tomorrow's power struggle between your group and the moderates.)

In any event, it is better to be a witness to rather than a recipient of the "brutality," as the case of Dwight Worker, a student at Indiana University, readily attests:

Dwight Worker was pulled from the couch by a stick
placed around the back of his neck, under the edge
of his helmet. On the floor, the back of his helmet
was pulled up and he was struck on the back of the
neck. About this time, Officer Branam was tripped
or fell over Worker's body; he and another officer
dragged Worker to the east side of the room, where
Branam got behind Worker, pulled his helmet up, and
struck him on the back of the neck. Worker kicked
at Branam and grabbed his stick; Branam dragged
Worker across the floor, twisted his stick loose,
pulled Worker's helmet up and (by his own and
photographic testimony) struck him once or twice in
the mouth with his fist. During this struggle,
Worker kicked repeatedly at the officers. Worker
was eventually dragged, semi-conscious, to the bus.
From there he was taken to jail, and spent about
three hours being booked, mugged, fingerprinted,
and in the drunk tank before being transferred to
the University Health Center. He remained there
for two days and was examined for fractures, brain
damage, and scalp injury. The discharge diagnosis
was contusion (bruise) with hematoma (a collection
of hemorrhages).[6]

Clearly, this climactic phase of confrontational strategy can be exciting—
but it can also be painful.

Part I of our *Manual* would not be complete if we failed to list two
additional phases, phases which may appear to be somewhat anticlimactic
and perhaps optional, but which should not be underrated because of their
brevity.

Demand Amnesty!

Remember, medical schools accept only B.A.s.

Start Planning for the Next Confrontation

The new administration will need to be tested in confrontation proficiency.
And with the thought of this new administration in mind, as well as to
provide a semblance of fairness and balance to our *Manual*, let's turn our
focus for a moment to Part II.

Timely Tips for the New-Style Administrator

1. *Cultivate a life style compatible with the more* avant garde *students.*
Whatever the new mode of dress, try to wear some slightly toned-down
version of it. Read "in" magazines like *Rolling Stone* to learn the latest
campus terminology. In the seventies it is "in" for administrators to be
brutally honest and to register their disapproval of anything with a tersely
uttered "Fuck." Another often-used expression is *heavy*, which substitutes
for groovy, deep, or meaningful: "The play tonight was heavy."

How do you get a job as an administrator?

2. *At minor disturbances, be conciliatory and appear to be on the side
of the students.* Climb into the occupied building with a supply of sandwiches
and Coke. (*Note:* Not beer.) Find yourself a prominent area in the sit-in,
mount a desk, and—sitting cross-legged—lead an open, sensitive discussion
on the failures of higher education. When the sit-in finally breaks up, give
everyone the peace sign and organize a clean-up committee.

3. *Try to defuse future confrontations by bringing important student
leaders into your administration.* There are many ambitious students among
the protesters, and they can usually be persuaded to join the team. One
rhetorical strategy that has proven useful is to say: "Listen, Jim, I know you
are loyal to SDS, but this is a chance to destroy the cancer from the inside.
After a year in the Dean's office, I'm sure, Yale Law School will be quite
interested . . ."

4. *Plan your responses as a series of gradual escalations.* Do not become
irritated with radicals' name-calling, and make your replies measured and
ingratiating: "The concerned students make me proud, for the first time,
to be affiliated with _____College." The next day, become a little less
supportive of the protesters and firmly state: "We need vigilant watchdogs
to check abuses at this institution, but I think we should practice reason."
Finally (and dramatically), reach the end of your patience and intemperately
assail the dissidents with their own epithets: "Fascist!" "Racist!" "Liar!"
"Traitor!" All of these labels are good. Avoid *Commie* (overworked) and
Bolshevik (strained). Currently the magic word is *Maoist*, which conjures up
images of millions of drug-crazed Red Chinese storming onto the San Diego
beaches. Denunciatory phrases that command attention on the six-o'clock
news include "crass vigilantes," "children of known Stalinists," "supercilious
or effete intellectuals," and "irresponsible street people."

If you are *really* cornered, as a last resort you might invoke the words
of a late Austrian painter/paperhanger who, in 1932, railed:

The streets of our country are in turmoil. The
universities are filled with students rebelling and
rioting. Communists are seeking to destroy our
country. Russia is destroying us with her might.
And the republic is in danger. Yes, danger from
within and without. We need law and order! Without
law and order our nation cannot survive.
                    --Adolf Hitler, campaign speech[7]

5. *Lay careful plans.* If in the final analysis confrontation seems inevitable, quietly notify the police, and with them work out the details as to the
best time and place for the bust. Ask the police to be as gentle as possible.
This foresight will stand you in good stead with the faculty-student
committee that is sure to be appointed after "differences" are settled.

LAW WILL PREVAIL

"I never thought I would see such a thing. It makes you sick to your stomach.

"But students must learn that law and order will prevail, and the sooner they learn it, the better off they are going to be.

"None of my men want to use clubs on anyone, particularly on young people.

"But in these situations, police are only human, and despite their high degree of training there are always some who will be provoked beyond their capacity to contain themselves."

—Boston Public
Safety Commissioner[8]

---

6. *Be your own man.* When the protesters finally break into your office
and threaten to carry you out, pick up a baseball bat and threaten: "The
first bastard who walks in will get his goddam head kicked in." The trustees
will like that.

7. *Announce a radical restructuring.* Possibly to forestall a confrontation, and certainly to save face, announce as a last-ditch effort that you are
radically restructuring the institution. Make the proposed changes as
sweeping and as innovative as possible. Quickly throw out grades and merge
the chemistry and classics departments. Then announce student-run seminars
and fire the provost. This is sure to split some of the moderates off from the
radicals. If your proposals are accepted—by trustees, faculty, and the student
body as a whole—you will be faced with a new and happier opportunity:
you can push through much-needed reform while, at the same time, getting
rid of incompetent retreads in the administration.

If, as a new administrator, you assiduously apply the foregoing principles,
hanging onto your job is your reward. In fact, you may be acclaimed a
savior of democracy, urged to run for public office, or even be invited to
write a daily column for a chain of newspapers. If, however, your counter-

confrontational strategies fail, you might be wise to have a few "feeler" letters out for a new position. These days, many colleges are looking for new-style administrators.

Confrontation Revisited

When public dialogue fails, frustrated and disillusioned people take up the strategy of confrontation. If the confrontation is successful, the people (on all sides) begin to talk about mutual problems.

I walked around campus, and there was every professor
I've ever had. They all had concerned expressions
on their faces, and they were there. I felt like
crying. . . . Four years of college, and it takes a
strike to get the professors out of the library.
                    --A Northwestern University co-ed,
                        commenting on the 1970 strike

During a confrontation, to separate truth from fiction is difficult. The extreme rhetoric turns you off—but the administration has lied and busted heads—so you listen to both sides and try to make a choice on inadequate evidence.

This commencement is an atrocity, an obscenity. . . .
Our interests as students do not lie in this tea
party with these criminals. . . . It lies in fighting them in alliance with the people, and we should
get out of here.
--SDS Commencement Speaker, Harvard University, 1969[9]

. . . it is my personal feeling that the students
who are trying to run the university rather than get
an education had better move on.
                    --Trustee, Ohio State University, 1962[10]

There is sadness in both confrontation and bomb-throwing, for they are testimony that democratic process has broken down and has become too remote and unresponsive to the will of the people.

The sovereignty of the United States resides in the
people, not in the machines, and it's the people's
to take back, if they so wish. "The machines," said
Paul, "have exceeded the personal sovereignty will-
ingly surrendered to them by the American people
for government. Machines and organization and

pursuit of efficiency have robbed the American
people of liberty and the pursuit of happiness."
                    --Kurt Vonnegut, Jr., <u>Player Piano</u>[11]

If, as some are already concluding, the student movement is dead, gone
to committee, what happened to educational change? Schools are still
impersonal. Famous professors remain inaccessible. The only dialogue is in
your room with a few friends. In retrospect, the efforts seem so noble and
justified, and yet so wasted.

A "rEVolutioN is not a SPECTACLE!

ThERe aRe NO SPECTAToRS!

EveRYoNe paRticipAtes WheThER tHeY KNoW it oR NoT

mad, bomber

Monday, August 24th at 3 a.m. the Army Math Research Center in Madison, Wisconsin was blown up. A researcher who was in the building working late was killed. The following leaflet, entitled "Why the Bombing" was issued soon after. It speaks for itself:

"We who understand and support the demolition of the Army Math Research Center must speak for ourselves because the official media have distorted the event beyond recognition.

"They do not tell you that this was not any mathematics research center solving any theoretical problems, but the nation's only Army math research center whose role is to solve military problems, to design triggers for others to pull.

"Their research has killed literally thousands of innocent people and has developed instruments for the delivery of nuclear and chemical-biological bombs.

"These researchers shield their eyes from the fact that their work is used to keep the privileged ruling minorities in power around the world, and the press terms this self-imposed blindness 'neutrality.'

"The media does not tell you that the bombers defended human life, not only by attacking an institution of organized murder but by choosing the least likely time of day and time of year when the building was to be occupied—and then by phoning their warning to police 12 minutes before the actual explosion.

"The police made no attempt to call the walkie-talkie equiped guards in the Army Math Building.

"They do not tell you the history that led reasonable people to commit acts of force. For a full year an increasing number of students attempted to expose the real function of Army Math and to shut it down.

"At first they tried persuasion, distributing thousands of pamphlets describing the different ways that the research services the needs of the military. This led to a student demand for negotiations, but the university administration refused to negotiate.

"Then followed seven months of futile protest, ranging from nonviolent marches last November to rock-throwing attacks this May. By ignoring reasoned argument and negotiation, the university's managers provoked rebellion.

"By responding to rebellion with naked force they left those who disagreed with only one option—force in return. This is the background for the bombing of the Army Math Research Center, the story the news media never covered.

"They do not tell you the facts that would explain the bombing and then they claim that there isn't an explanation, that it was the act of a 'twisted mind.'

"But we are not lunatics and our actions are not wanton. We want to live and we want to be free and if the military suppresses life and freedom then we must suppress the military."

signed,

LIFE ABOVE THE TREES

5 Sticks and Stones: The Language of Dissent

Sticks and stones
May break my bones,
But words can
Never hurt me.

—Childhood Chant

The language of dissent can be heard on all sides, often raucously, sometimes seductively. It uses highly volatile words, reversed meanings, and exaggerations. Many parents in America would no doubt welcome a translation of this linguistic twisting:

```
Hump the Hump/Off the Pigs/Kill a Commie for Christ/
Make Love, Not War/Shoot a Motherfucker Tonight.
```

But definition and identification are only a part of the significance of protest language. When a dissident dislikes a political or social system, he finds it increasingly objectionable to use its linguistic code. His rejection of the conventional communicative code produces a number of interesting language variations and derivative alterations. These changes and deviations can loosely be called the language of dissent.

```
The obscenity helped define our struggle.  Finally,
we could say in public what we had been saying
among ourselves.  We could use our own language.
All forms of authority, tradition, respect (you
show respect, obviously, by not using your own
language) had broken down.
```
                                                        --Mark Rudd[1]

In the preceding chapter, we noted briefly how invective, epithets, and other shock words are used by protesters to throw officials off balance during verbal and physical confrontation. In this chapter, we want to take a somewhat broader and longer look at operational linguistics, noticing in particular some of the ways in which volatile, abusive, or insidious language is used both to *attack* and *defend* the status quo.

One tendency in recent decades has been to view our society *divisively,* as if it had been halved into two camps: the Have's and the Have-Not's, or the Possessors and the Dispossessed, or—in our immediate times—the Establishment and the Anti-Establishment. Members of the latter camp generally prefer to be called protesters or dissenters. However, this kind of division is too easy, too simple; and one of its major flaws is that it often fails to recognize to any real, operational extent a vast uncommitted "middle" segment. Sometime prior to the 1968 presidential campaign, Richard Nixon and his advisers sensed that there must be a significantly large segment of the country's population that did not classify itself as *either* Establishment or Anti-Establishment. And to this segment, the so-called Silent Majority, they programmed an important part of their election campaign. This chapter will take into account, as a consequence, both the vocal minority and majority.

For our purposes, we will use the term *dissent* to mean *disagree*; and by *dissenter* we will mean one who disagrees not necessarily with the majority view, but rather with a *current* view that is being loudly or violently or seductively expressed, even if those expressing it represent only a comparatively small portion of the population.

Under this situational umbrella, we can examine "differing" or dissentive language—whether it is being used by a dean or a student, a Republican or a Democrat, a churchman or an atheist, a Jerry Rubin or a Spiro T. Agnew. In our special context, each such "voice" would be opposing something or somebody, and each would be seeking the most effective linguistic artillery with which to criticize, put down, or annihilate the view, stance, integrity, or credibility of his opponent.

Nattering Nabobs of Negativism

The use of deprecatory language to disarm or immobilize an adversary is nothing new in man's history. Cain no doubt initiated his lethal assault on Abel in this way; in fact, the Serpent quite probably used it against Adam when he was whispering into Eve's ear. What is new is the savage determination with which dissentive language has been employed. The intensity of the feelings and actions to be evoked from one's adversary can be gauged with a fair amount of accuracy, depending upon the selection of the language: obscenity, invective, or subtle derogation.

There are two main classes of dissentive language: *deprecation* and *obscenity*. Although both of these categories are often interrelated, to break them down is useful for definitional purposes.

Deprecation

Deprecatory language may include obscenities, but often it stands by itself and takes many forms. The mainstream of deprecation is *invective*, which is characterized by bitter denunciation and is usually *vituperative* and *abusive*. "Dean Smith is a murderer" is a typical example.

Used less frequently but more effectively are various forms of *ridicule*, which are a subcategory of deprecation. Simple forms of ridicule include pointedly mispronouncing a dignitary's name, misusing his title, calling him by his first name, and a variety of other strategic insults: "President Hickson," "Mayor Garbage," "Bloody Dicky." The put-on can be an obvious form of ridicule, as are satire and much of parody. When the demonstrators start shouting, "We love you, Dean Smith," most sophisticated observers have reason to be suspicious.

Obscenity

Obscene language is generally defined as *lewd, repulsive,* or *disgusting* utterances. According to Ashley Montagu, obscenity is "a form of swearing that makes use of indecent words and phrases."[2] The classic obscene word is *fuck*, and its mere mention in any number of contexts and variations can cause blind fury and riots. Try shouting "Fuck Dean Smith" in his presence and find out how fast he responds.

Often deprecation and obscenity are combined in a single event. For example, groups like the San Francisco Mime Troupe* might satirize campus

---

*The San Francisco Mime Troupe is a guerrilla theater group which specializes in lampooning political figures and events.

unrest or stage demonstrations which involve the Yippies or similar groups by declaring: "Dean Jones treats the motherfucking, piggish hippies like scum, and that's why we are honoring him today as American of the Year."

The Function of the Language of Dissent

Rhetorical critic Robert L. Scott observes that "obscenity helps perform at least three necessary functions":[3]

1. It gains attention.
2. It puts in perspective the hypocrisies of contemporary society.
3. Vocally, it is the ultimate expression of aggressive hostility.

These three purposes can be extended to include the language of dissent.

The attention-getting function of dissentive language is its obvious *shock value*. While the word *fuck* and its derivative *motherfucker* create instant attention, so do *fascist, pig,* and other terms of derogation. In fact, almost any word or phrase not in currently "acceptable" use or out of appropriate context is likely to engender attention.

The argument that deprecatory language puts a number of hypocrisies in perspective is persuasive. Dissenters argue that while Americans commit the most heinous crimes for the flag or for money, they consider the use of four-letter words or invective a worse crime. The rebels also are fond of pointing out that *hate* and *kill* are permissible words, whereas *fuck* and certain uses of the word *pig* are banned. Repetition of the offending words or phrases puts the inconsistencies into perspective for some writers. Consider the question: "What's obscene—*fuck* or *draft*?"

D***t: A Parable

Once upon a time, there was a beautiful chick. One day, she went on a demonstration at a local draft board. She carried a sign which read: FUCK THE DRAFT. All the secretaries at the local draft board screamed a little when they saw the beautiful chick's sign. So a recruiting sergeant with a strong stomach went up to the beautiful chick and asked her please to censor her sign, because the local draft board secretaries . . . well, you know. So the beautiful chick dug what the sergeant was saying. She left the picket line and disappeared. A little while later, she came back, and now her sign read: FUCK THE D***T.

—*Peace and Freedom News*[4]

That deprecatory language is *aggressive* and *hostile* is fairly obvious.

Later in the chapter we will describe a police officer's reaction to obscenities and deprecations. In our society, we are "programmed" to fight when we are confronted with abusive language. "No one can call me that" or "Take that back, you son of a bitch" are typical and, to some, gentlemanly responses. Somehow, unless we retort in kind, the words and phrases stick to us and hurt, partly because we recognize that the abuser means us harm.

Situations and Strategies

Typically, in situations calling for linguistic choice and offensive finesse, an authority symbol (mayor, judge, president, warden, principal, dean) is in the position of withholding a certain institutional prerogative which a challenging group wants to share. The strategies for using deprecatory language and its variations in such circumstances might be explained thus:

How to End a Meeting

Abusive language composes the perfect argument for the dissenter. The beauty of the obscenity-and-invective attack rests in the ineffectiveness of the adversary's retort.

RADICALS: *(in unison.)* PIG! PIG! FASCIST! FASCIST!
MAYOR: Let me answer the first comment first. I am not a pig. Do I look like a pig?
RADICALS: *(in unison; jeeringly.)* YEAH! YEAH!
MAYOR: *(trying to shout above the interruption.)* As to the second comment, let me affirm that I am not . . . and never will be . . . a fascist.

Had the radical attacked the authority figure on some substantive issue, the latter might be able to marshal facts and figures to counter the charges. But when an argument is fought at the level of abusiveness, it usually ends in frustration and bitterness for the peacemakers. And how do you argue with an obscenity—with another obscenity? "Fuck you!" "Fuck you, too!!" The culmination of the exchange often is an abrupt conclusion of the meeting, or additional hard feelings. Certainly, there is little efficient problem-solving. Frequently, for the dissenter the truncated meeting is a favorable outcome since the deprecatory attack has the virtue of slowing down the negotiating process to allow late supporters to join the cause. When some substantive issues are being resolved, the dirty-word attack often is employed to sabotage the potential of the deliberations.

Just Call Me John

Another category of this particular language ploy is the disarming of an adversary by calling him by his first name. If the mayor of Newark is addressed by the dissenters as "John," and the director of job placement as "Murray," it is quarrelsome and unegalitarian for these two power figures to protest the impropriety and presumptuousness of such informalities. In addition, any pleading for due respect is likely to be reproduced in a derisive, mimeographed handout which eventually makes its way into the mass media:

GOVERNOR JOHNSON OBJECTS TO BEING CALLED PHILLIP!

Local sources claim that Governor C. Phillip Johnson flew into a rage when called "Phillip" by protesting state policemen. The Governor was alleged to have shouted to an assistant: "I HATE THE NAME PHILLIP!"

This kind of publicity is not welcomed by officials at any level. More-over, because of its potential humor, such an incident is inevitably used as a feature story or as a closing "laugh" line on the six-o'clock newscast. Furthermore, the official is less likely to argue about having his name used with premeditated casualness by the dissenter when there are other and much more important issues at stake. Quibbling about the use of a first name pales before the issues of integrated housing or better schools.

Considerable momentary advantage accrues to the dissenter who, in an abrasive context, calls an administrator by his first name. The tactic places the untitled on an equal footing with the authority; it levels the latter by blatantly ignoring his rank. It is a lot easier for a dissident to be outrageous or nasty when addressing a linguistically defrocked official. There is some-thing compulsively civilizing about titles of rank. They maintain distance between people. To bridge or narrow this distance breaks down formality and contributes to intimacy, and the power of authority to maintain order is decreased. If a dissenter preserves decorum, he stands in danger of promoting and facilitating the negotiating relationships of father to child, leader to follower, ordained minister to lay churchman. The challenger, therefore, attempts to break the pattern by, first, stripping away the natural rhetorical advantage of the authority and, second, selecting language aimed at unsettling or leveling the one being challenged.

This language ploy, although initially highly effective, is not without its trap. While it may for the moment lock the challenged authority figure into an untenable position, over the long term it will likely work to the disadvantage of the dissenter as well. When true negotiating begins, few wish to deal with those who have been disrespectful—or with anyone else who has been muddied by the "sordid affair." A likely outcome of the taunting encounter is that the final bargaining will have to come from a second and less antagonistic group or leadership. The harassed official quite likely will be replaced by a higher-echelon figure, and the offensive and abusive protesters will be relieved by less sullied negotiators. Thus, name-calling protesters and besieged officials alike frequently are mere cannon fodder in the linguistic wars. The final advantages are usually inherited by the second group of protesters; the original dissidents often end on the suspended list, and the beleaguered official frequently finds himself seeking employment elsewhere.

Exactly What Do You Mean?

The put-on is another language tactic used effectively by dissenters. As noted in Chapter 1 ("The Put-On"), this linguistic device is all-pervasive and quite deadly at close range. In the special context of dissent, the put-on is used to befuddle, irritate, and—as in the case of strategies discussed earlier—slow down the negotiating process. One such instance was a dignified Harvard graduation ceremony where a student, speaking in Latin, saluted President Nathan Pusey for having defended the University against "anarchy and demagoguery"[5] during the strike of 1969. Another example was the counter put-on staged by students protesting the action of the dissenters. Instead of arguing the issues, the nonactivists parodied SDS demands:

> **END UNIVERSAL EXPANSION**: For a great many years now, the universe has been rapidly expanding, having in this enterprise the full co-operation of the Harvard Astronomy Department. This expansion is unfair in that the big, fat Elliptical Galaxies have all the time been indiscriminately mopping up the small, poor Irregular Galaxies, using all kinds of physical force. This same force is used in earthquakes to displace working people from their homes. We demand that the Astronomy Department reverse this policy, and that they turn over their labs and observatories to relocation centers run by us until this is done.
> —Anonymous handbill[6]

In the first example, the commencement speaker created ambiguity about his purpose among the thousands who were listening, and in the second example the anonymous pamphleteers were ridiculing the alleged pretense of the SDS. In both cases, however, the dissenters were taking minimal risk because the put-on is a relatively safe device and one which, unlike some of the other linguistic strategies, enables the executioner to maintain a low profile. The intent of the put-on artist is rarely clear, and therefore the adversary's response is frequently measured and tentative, rather than bold or violent. But, like the other strategies, it does attack and sometimes exposes the power lust of an opposing group.

Why Deprecation Works

If people merely laughed off the obscenity or invective when attacked, the needling practice would terminate. For the dissenter, the joy of deprecation springs from the temporary instability and passion of the deprecated. Take away that advantage, and the dissenters would have to find new weapons.

The day of termination, however, seems distant. Many people have difficulty in responding to abusive and volatile language because it offends certain codes. For some, this reaction borders on prudery. After all, one does not deal with people who use foul language, does one?

In an informal interview with a police officer after the Columbia riot, author Roger Kahn transcribed the kind of responses that reinforce the offensiveness of foul language for a large number of people. Speaking confidentially to the author, the police officer recalled a particular scene. In refusing to be moved from a particular area, a dissenting co-ed reacted to the officer's order by saying "Your sister sucks off your mother." The officer, recalling his blind fury, told Kahn: "So I hit her. I hit her good. I made her cry."[7] The policeman's response was understandable, but it is also testimony to the inability of many people to remain calm when they are the target of obscenity. Even the police—who, when they enlist, agree to take a certain amount of abuse—find it difficult to restrain themselves. "But I got limits. My mother doesn't have to take abuse."[8]

Your Limits?

If you're a little squeamish . . .

```
Maybe Jerry Lewis would go on television, and
instead of getting hung up with muscular dystrophy,
he'd have a clap-a-thon.
                              --Lenny Bruce[9]
```

If you're slightly "stout" . . .

FATTY FATTY TWO BY FOUR
CAN'T GET THRU THE KITCHEN DOOR.

—Kids

If you're religious . . .

```
The indignant Goldwater Republicans immediately
rendered John Lindsay the inestimable service of
opposing him with a list of ultras under the direc-
tion of that same William Buckley who a short time
ago called good Pope John "that fellow-traveling
foreigner."
     --La Tribune de Genève, Geneva, July 23, 1965.¹⁰
```

A Romance: Media and Dissenters

The use of deprecating language receives tremendous media coverage, and this factor makes deprecation work. Media find the obscenities and the volatile language irresistible. Television, in particular, has proved itself most effective when covering tense, unpredictable events. Often the shouting matches generate a suspenseful atmosphere which is compact and suitable for capsule television summaries.

Because of the time restriction of a one-minute news presentation, the television editor is obligated to select the most dramatic displays for inclusion. Actually, the meeting or confrontation may have been dominated by qualified speakers offering reasoned discourse on conflicting issues; but the television editor, because of priorities, does not have time to include the detailed discourse if he is to capture the excitement and drama of the event. He therefore selects the unisonous shouts to fulfill his needs because, although they may distort the event, they prevent listeners from turning to another channel.

Making for even greater hypocrisy is the media's censoring of the obscenities. Ethel Grodzins Romm reported that during the 1968 Chicago Democratic Convention "Sieg Heil!" and "Pigs!" and "Hump the Hump" came over the air, but not "Motherfucker!" and "Cocksucker!"¹¹ Television directors commonly turn down the volume for obscenities and raise it for invectives. This censorship is evident also in the daily newspapers when "Fuck Daley" is reported as "Down with Daley" or some other euphemism. The United States Criminal Code does prohibit the use or utterance of obscene, indecent, or profane language, but the media's interpretation of the Code is capricious and obviously opportunistic.

Deprecation as Therapy

And, finally, it simply "feels good" to swear. The release of an oath is a powerful agent for mental health. Though mothers have been claiming for years that swearing is bad and can turn a thirteen-year-old's hair to gray . . . it still feels good. The college president who is the target of a series of scathing epithets usually is not aware of the therapeutic function he serves.

Alan Katzman, co-editor of *The Village Other*, affirms this beneficial effect:

```
The last time I swore was in the Army.  But now I
feel just the same way I felt in the Army.  All
organizations with tight disciplines are the same
way.  Chicago cops were worse swearers than the Army
sergeants.  It's feeling repressed in a repressed
society.  You need the words for release.¹²
```

The Guardians of God-Given Goodness: A Real-Life Example

One politician who understands the power of language is Spiro Agnew. As Vice-President, Agnew uses a number of deprecatory language devices to protest a minority view—his definition of "minority" being anyone not in accord with the incumbent party. Himself a dissident by our definition of the word, he began his linguistic barrage, modestly enough, with mere double alliteratives such as "vicars of vacillation" and "pusillanimous pussy-footing," moved quickly to such quadruple sets as "hopeless, hysterical hypochondriacs of history," and finally graduated to euphonious successions typified by "a paralyzing permissiveness pervades every policy." It is as if alliteration were the answer to the attacks of other dissidents. However, it would be a mistake to assume that Agnew limits himself to a single rhetorical device; he is more versatile than that. To his public pronouncements he has also added a "vocal shorthand": "radiclibs" (radical-liberals), "troglodytic leftists" (cave-seeking radicals), "sheep in wolves' clothing" (opponents who switch stands before election), and "The Come Lately Club" (tardy law-and-order supporters). In fact, his critics sometimes accuse the Vice-President of trying to quash criticism of the Nixon administration under a trainload of rhetorical figures.

If Agnew's linguistic devices are not the most stylish, they nonetheless have the virtue of memorability. This is rather surprising in view of the fact that he delivers his collection of rhetorical flourishes with little animation or emotion. Only occasionally does he show irritability or anger, as when—for example—after taking a nasty heckling, he imitated an orchestra conductor and proceeded to direct an imaginary symphony to the rhythm of his adversaries' chants. Once, when particularly aggravated, he responded with "You're pathetic." But this is rare. Usually, his delivery is that of a genial Rotarian who smiles tightly, grits his teeth, and doggedly battles his way through the speech.

The impact of Agnew's linguistic assaults should not be underestimated. His provocative phrasing and convincing charges attract newscasters and make headlines. Whether in Des Moines or Miami, every time Spiro comes up with a new alliteration the television networks and the nation's press give it the broadest possible coverage. While some of this attention may have been born out of fear following the Vice-President's attack on the biases of the media, even his enemies would probably admit that most of the coverage is earned. If, in a given instance, his speech is composed of twenty-nine minutes of turgid prose and sixty seconds of catchy homilies, the sixty-seconds burst is shrewdly tailored to television. The media can almost invariably expect the one-minute flourish; and since that is probably all they can use anyway, they are well content—and so is the Vice-President. The Des Moines audience may find the "live" speech disappointing, but the immediate listeners are merely a frame for reaching millions more through the media. Agnew may be the first major political figure who not only uses but also *understands* the realities of media coverage. His ability to speak colorfully and memorably in one-minute bursts for the benefit of six-o'clock newscasts is striking evidence of that understanding.

Another admitted advantage to the Agnew alliterative barrage is that it prevents effective counterattacks from opponents. And this, as we have seen, is one of the dissenter's most potent strategies. Those detractors who insist that Spiro's witticisms are undergirded by a clownish quality which is hard to take seriously would have to agree that this brand of barbed humor is difficult to answer. Worse, it can be punishing. In the parlance of the prize-fight, instead of a steady stream of jabs and hooks, he loops a roundhouse right that occasionally connects. Agnew's lack of consistency makes him a difficult man to counter; and coupled with his wide television exposure, it makes him a dangerous man to antagonize.

```
We tell the people we work with that if Agnew comes
into their state, don't tangle with him.  Just lie
low and let him pass.
          --Eastern Pollster with Democratic Clients13
```

One of the factors that make Agnew's dissentive language effective is that he refrains from using obscenity. The Vice-President employs cute phraseology that can be nasty, but is never obscene. Since he represents the office of the President and is also an elected official, he cannot be overly abusive or offensive. But Agnew—and his followers—no doubt feel that since he is giving his adversaries "a taste of their own medicine" he has all of the license and justification he needs to abuse his opponents. And to make his thrusts even more telling, his comments are generally cute, yet biting and satirical, and the public conduct of his targets quite often substantiates his charges.

The Agnew verbal strategies suffer from the same disadvantages as those of other dissenters. Admittedly, he ably draws the political fire away from Richard Nixon—a service Nixon performed for Dwight Eisenhower during the fifties. The Vice-President also serves well as the public scold for the major issues his party wishes to pursue: Law and Order, Honorable Withdrawal from Vietnam, Recovery of Domestic Economy, and so on. However, the role of stirring up strong feelings with entertaining phrases can easily end in personal disaster for the phrase-maker. The populace likes to place its confidence in less volatile, less partisan public figures. Thus, Agnew—like some of the more abusive radicals—is potentially cannon fodder. A valuable man, he may find that in the end he, too, is expendable.

The use of deprecatory language has limited value. Momentarily, it may attract wide public attention and vast media exposure for the user; but frequently, in the final counting, it reduces or destroys his capability to negotiate and locks him out of power. To be really accurate, then, the chant of our childhood should be slightly altered:

Sticks and stones
May break your bones,
But words can
***Really* hurt you.**

6 I'll Get You, Professor

Why do students heckle? Are they mere usurpers, "gangsters of the left," obnoxious children? Hardly. Psychologist Kenneth Keniston has pointed out their superior academic achievement, altruism, and maturity.[1] But they do have an inability to ask the great questions, the questions of a metaphysical nature which undergird our society. The academic establishment is concerned with technological questions and has ingrained in its charges the same penchant for predication and control. Students can scarcely be expected, therefore, to transcend this training and revise our conception of truth and knowledge. As a consequence, they retreat to a gut reaction.

They look at the war, the ghettos, the increasing reaction of right-wing and liberal forces of "law and order," and they feel indignation.

> --Michael Novak, Commonweal[2]

Many students criticize professors for insensitivity to their needs. They claim that the average professor teaches his three to twelve hours per week, attends an occasional faculty meeting, and then retreats to his home for gardening and cocktail parties. He doesn't appear to live the life of a person dedicated to the pursuit of truth or to the general welfare of his students. He seems less than a human being as, amidst revolution and turmoil, he lectures about Dryden and never asks of himself the great questions: Why is there a gap between the professional disciplines and the real world? What are the sources of his distortions, value judgments, political biases, economic status, and professional commitments? In various ways, the students are turning upon this rather complacent and powerful member of society and asking for an accounting. They would like to see professors serve as more of a model for students, to compel them to reexamine the very language and values of academe. One of the specific means by which they try to accomplish this is the heckle.

The Heckle: Student as Fox

Probably heading the students' list of most deserving targets is the inadequacies of the lecture as a communication medium. The lecturer, wired for sound and delivering his carefully written notes to 545 numbered students, is a frequent and invariably predominant figure in thousands of classrooms. This medium for disseminating knowledge is justified by college administrators because (a) it reduces the per capita cost of education, and (b) under ideal conditions it permits the students to hear and benefit from the presumed wisdom of a great man. Regardless of the rationale, however, the system does breed *impersonalization*. And for many students caught in what seems a manipulative and impersonal society, the lecture method is degrading.

As a defensive outcry against injustices and inequities, to whatever extent they may be real, students resort to the heckle—a rhetorical strategy designed to fluster and anger the professor. The student who decides to "get" the professor waits for an opportune time in the lecture, and then attacks. He may, for instance, yell "Bullshit" at a particularly opinionated point. Or he may counter the professor's argument with a stream of references: "That's not what Bronkowski says," or "Have you read 'Howl'?" A variation is to use the obscure reference: "Did you read _____?" The question is asked in a mocking manner with a cute, upturned inflection at the end. An interesting rhetorical feature of the heckle is that the roles of professor and student are—at the insistence of the student—reversed by using many of the tactics that the academicians themselves characteristically employ: scorn or heavy sarcasm bordering on the insult, false erudition, and copious references. What follows is a portion of actual dialogue taken from a communication theory class:

PROFESSOR: Let me place this communication model on the blackboard. *(He proceeds to draw the model.)*

STUDENT: What's it good for?

PROFESSOR: Well . . .

STUDENT: Bullshit. *(Nervous laughter from class.)*

PROFESSOR: I think eventually we will be able to predict certain kinds of strategies before they occur.

STUDENT: *(Shouting.)* So you can control our behavior and our lives?

PROFESSOR: If you'll allow me to finish, I'll be glad to answer . . .

ANOTHER STUDENT:
    You are finished.

OTHER CLASS MEMBERS:
    (After some sparse laughter.) Give him a chance. Come on. (Etc.)

PROFESSOR: I wasn't serious about the model (put-on). It's not my model (cop-out).

The exchange between the professor and the students contains a number of important communication hazards. The alienation that some students feel toward the academic environment can produce not only a disrespectful unmasking of the professor, but it also serves to dissipate the empathy and increase the likelihood of alienation between the professor and his *other* students. Not unlike the confrontational strategy in which authority figures are put down by being called "Jim" instead of "Mayor" or "Governor," the heckle corrodes the unique alliance that must exist between professor and students. And this, in turn, impairs the educational process and may even bring it to a complete standstill. The professor operates under an unofficial but nevertheless binding contract with his charges. The student comes to class, listens, takes notes, and is prepared to recognize the intellectual superiority of his teacher. Once this contract is broken by students, the university is in a precarious position because educational institutions are particularly vulnerable to this kind of fracture. Small groups of heckling demonstrators, using hit-and-run guerrilla tactics, can disrupt educative communication much more effectively than they can by occupying campus buildings. As the success of heckling at Berkeley and Harvard so clearly illustrates, there is little that a university can do to defend itself against this strategy. In both institutions, classroom efforts were reduced to shouting matches among hecklers, other students, and professors.

What factors make a particular professor a target of hecklers?

A professor, if quick, often can handle the individual heckler. Several retorts might be used in the face of this protest strategy. The first is to smash the student's attack with an incredible display of vituperation:

"Get the hell out of my classroom."

"I paid my tuition."

"Then get out and get your money back. I don't need this kind of hassle."

This strategy is effective when the class members are highly motivated to learn, and will support the professor. They *could* all walk out.

A second strategy is: "Okay, *you* teach the subject." Here, the professor sits back and lets the disruptive student lecture and lead the class discussion. There is the possibility that the student will be superb. Many of the subjects handled by today's "relevant" professor (blues, group behavior, drugs) are well within the purview of precocious undergraduates. But if the professor is the only living expert on the use of the pronoun "I" in Tennessee Williams' *Camino Real* . . .

A third professorial counterstrategy is: "I'm hurt. So feel sorry for me." The teacher throws himself on the mercy of the class and reminds the students of how tough a business teaching is today, but how he—notwithstanding—has devoted years of his life to it. This tactic is most effective when it is accompanied by a sincere voice, well-placed pauses, and a brave "but-I'll-carry-on" posture. Many professors who use the first strategy reluctantly, and cannot bring themselves to employ the second, consider the third—the "mournful martyr"—an almost foolproof ploy.

Variations: Student as Roadrunner

There are of course variations on the "I'll Get You, Professor" strategy, all of them bearing a resemblance to the heckle. One such variation might be called the "Unhappy Speech." In a happy, intellectually growing classroom, a student makes a speech about how the class is unhappy, chaotic, and stunted. Class members argue with the student speaker about his interpretation, and they are apparently victorious:

"I'm happy."

"I love it."

"You don't understand."
"Professor Smith is relevant."

During the following few days, the class becomes increasingly self-conscious about "having fun" and "growing." Productive involvement and optimism dissipate and, in fact, very soon are replaced by melancholy, discontent, quibbling, violent argument, and—finally—neurotic behavior.

To counter this student strategy, the professor asks the "unhappy" speech-maker to suggest ways for class improvement. The suggestions are usually so vacuous that the pessimistic criticism is ridiculed and then forgotten.

Does a heckler feel guilty?

A less subtle strategy for "getting the professor" is the creation of noisy or physical disturbance in the class. In order to create the necessary distractions, the students will engage in such typical activities as making provocative gestures to each other or to the professor, stripping off their clothing, and carrying on such additional acts of harrassment as whispering loudly, dropping pencils, coughing in chorus, and even playing cards or throwing dice. The purpose of the disturbances is to force the instructor to attend to these distracting activities and abandon the lecture. Among the most successful practitioners of this strategy were the three students who jumped up from time to time during the class period and insisted upon taking pictures of the lecturing professor. The poor pedagogue, trying to carry on amidst the blinding bursts of flashbulbs and the insistent requests of "just one more" (to say nothing of the general admixture of consternation, hilarity, and confusion), could barely finish.

In countering this tactic, the professor has several options open to him, among them:

Get out of town.
Sell cars.
Get a research grant.
Send spouse to lecture next time.

Decide to have a baby.
Become a dean.
Go back to school and heckle.

The heckle, whatever its form or variation, is a potent instrument. The strategy and the means used to counter it are almost always cruel and educationally barren. The heckler, his face often lost in the crowd, needn't reveal his true identity or actual purpose as he seeks an effective release for his aggressions. The strategy doesn't require the user to justify his comment, to employ reason, to extend himself or others intellectually. For the heckled, the tactic can mean deep embarrassment or swift triumph. The professor must be clever, ever ready with a number of put-downs; and then, if his counterattack works, he may be able to make his point. But after such a tortured battle for expression, the point is hardly worth making.

How They Did It

"They talk about me not being on the legitimate.
Why, lady, nobody's on the legit when it comes down
to cases; you know that."

—Al Capone[1]

"People are like china. They look beautiful, but
if you examine them closely you can find flaws.
When you turn on the heat, they crack."

—Irving J. Tressler, <u>How to Lose
Friends and Alienate People</u>[2]

"It's been advertised lately, in the last six
months or so, in <u>Time</u>, <u>Life</u>, <u>Look</u>, <u>Good House-
keeping</u>, and <u>Parents' Magazine</u>. It's also on TV.
It's used as a prize in those daytime giveaway
shows on television. You've seen it on 'Art Link-
letter,' 'Jeopardy,' and programs like that. You
don't watch daytime shows? Well, nobody does. I
don't blame you—I don't like that kind of stuff
either. Now this set is not yet on sale in the
sense that you could pick it up in a book store or
department store. But we do plan to have a
regular professional sales drive in this area in
about five or six months. Now, before that and in
addition to the national advertising, like I told
you, we are doing a lot of local advertising. Now
what this involves for me is going around and
talking to families. . . ."

—Strategies of an encyclopedia salesman

"Blacks must develop their own heroic images. To
the white boy, Garvey was a failure—to us he was
perfect for his time and context. To the white
boy Malcolm X was a hate teacher—to us he was the
highest form of Black Manhood in his generation."

—Maulana Ron Karenga[3]

When I was a kid, ice cream was a nickle a cone.
Now I can buy a smaller cone for a quarter. I
swear, 31 Flavors, when you go to a buck a cone, I
will stop eating ice cream.

"Roy, I would give my whole life to win this game and take the pennant. Promise me that you will go in there and do your damndest."
  "I will go in," Roy sighed.

--Bernard Malamud, <u>The Natural</u>[4]

"What! Found your mittens,
You good little kittens?
Then you shall have some pie."
"Purr, purr, purr, purr,
    Purr, purr, purr, purr."

—"Three Little Kittens"

"I have never, I think, gotten such joy and satisfaction from a course. I simply gobbled up everything, the class sessions, the reading, the relationships that developed."

--College student to professor

"We hold these truths to be self-evident: That all men are created equal; that they are endowed by their Creator with certain inalienable rights; that among these are life, liberty, and the pursuit of happiness."

--Declaration of Independence

HOT LUNCH MENU

MONDAY
  Spaghetti and meat hot dish, green beans, cookies, peanut butter and plain sandwiches and milk.

TUESDAY
  Mashed potatoes, gravy, meat loaf, buttered carrots, prunes, plain sandwiches and milk.

WEDNESDAY
  Chili, crackers, carrot sticks, bar, plain sandwiches and milk.

THURSDAY
  Baked beans with ham, pickles, peanut butter and plain sandwiches and milk.

FRIDAY
  Weiner winks, corn, chocolate frosty creme dessert, plain sandwiches and milk.

A smile is often a bridge to friendship!

DEAR SOMEBODY: There are always people who think
THEY are superior to others less fortunate. I don't
think a "big" nose and a "poor" personality are
necessarily unattractive. Learn to smile and ask
your parents to let you have a nose job.

                    --Newspaper columnist's advice

"(1) The work situation. We saw that the [pool]
hustler must be not only a skilled player, but that
he must be skilled at pretending not to have great
playing skill. The latter requirement is one thing
that distinguishes him from the usual con man (who
often, on the contrary, feigns more expertise than
he has). And it also distinguishes him from the
usual professional gambler. The latter indeed
sometimes pretends to be other than he is and dis-
claims real skill ('I guess I'm just lucky tonight'),
but he relies basically on playing skill alone, or
else on a combination of playing with cheating
skill--being able to switch dice into and out of a
game, or to deal seconds or thirds or bottom cards,
etc. Pretending to lack of skill is not a basic
requirement of the gambler's job, as it is for the
hustler. As far as I know, this hustling reliance
on competence at feigning incompetence is unique,
and nowhere treated in the occupational literature."

        --Ned Polsky, Hustlers, Beats, and Others[5]

"I was to learn later in life that we tend to meet
any new situation by reorganizing; and a wonderful
method it can be for creating the illusion of
progress while producing confusion, inefficiency,
and demoralization."

        --from Petronius Arbiter (circa AD 60)[6]

Preface
Number Two

This book was not written for money. I have decided to forego any monetary profits and donate all cash to the Lumels of America. The Lumels are a not-for-profit organization devoted to helping kids from low-income families relocate in a meaningful Saturday program of therapy. In fact, this program has proven so successful that thirteen million low-income children are now making their way in a world much more verdant.

The publisher, who ordinarily loves money, has decided to throw in all ink used in the production of this book and thereby to make the manufacturing costs more reasonable, thus enabling the Lumels to realize more profit.

To my wife, I promise not to give away my next book. Please come home.

Irving J. Rein
Northwestern University

HOW THEY SAY IT

SECTION TWO

MANIPULATION, REDEFINITION, SIS, BOOM AND BAH, COMMUNICATION SYSTEMS, COMMUNICATION SYSTEMS, RAH, RAH, RAHLLL!

IN THE LAST FIFTY YEARS, THE COMMUNICATION INSTRUMENTS OF MODERN SOCIETY HAVE UNDERGONE MAJOR CHANGES, AND ONLY NOW ARE WE BEGINNING TO SENSE THE VAST IMPLICATIONS OF WHAT HAS BEEN AND IS PRESENTLY TAKING PLACE. THESE CHANGES, IN NO SMALL PART, HAVE GROWN OUT OF TECHNICAL INNOVATIONS RANGING FROM THE TELEPHONE TO TELEVISION. IN ADDITION, BECAUSE OF MEDIA, FORMS OF COMMUNICATION WHICH HAD LITTLE IMPACT DURING THE EARLY PART OF OUR COUNTRY'S HISTORY NOW HAVE GREAT POWER. SOME NEWER FORMS ARE FOLK AND ROCK MUSIC, POETRY, GRAFFITI, COMEDY ACTS AND HAPPENINGS.

URBAN BLUES, FOR EXAMPLE, WE WILL VIEW AS COMMUNICATIVE RITUAL AND NOT AS SECULAR ENTERTAINMENT. WE WILL TAKE A LOOK AT ROCK RADIO NOT SIMPLY AS ROCK MUSIC, BUT AS A FLOW OF DAILY EXISTENCE. WE WILL SCRUTINIZE MOVIES AS MYTH AND NOT MERE EMOTIONAL ESCAPE...

AND **I'LL** SHOW YOU THAT GRAFFITI IS NOT MERE SCRIBBLING BUT A COMPLEX COMMUNICATION SYSTEM.

EACH ONE OF THESE PRESENTATIONAL FORMS IS TRYING TO COMMUNICATE THE IDEAS AND ATTITUDES OF CERTAIN PEOPLE TO CERTAIN OTHER PEOPLE. AT THE SAME TIME, WE WILL NOT LOSE SIGHT OF THE NOTION THAT THE COMMUNICATION WHICH TAKES PLACE IS VERY OFTEN DISGUISED UNDER A SOMETIMES EXCEEDINGLY THIN VENEER OF ENTERTAINMENT, THUS MAKING ITS APPEAL SUBTLE AND, SIMULTANEOUSLY INCREASING ITS EFFECTIVENESS.

7 The Rhetoric of Popular Arts

The popular arts always have been persuasive. Whether a comedy by George Bernard Shaw or a waltz by Johann Strauss, a Western by Howard Hawks or a comic monologue by Will Rogers, they have worked attitude changes. In extreme cases, such an art may have effected change in a political belief; more often, it has created an alteration in a personal view or conviction. What is noteworthy about persuasion-in-art today is that through technological innovation one presentation—a single song, a single dramatic performance—can be appreciated by millions of people. Before the introduction of electronic media, the opportunity for the masses to witness a play or hear a musical concert was slim. Such enjoyment was a luxury which the average wage earner could not afford; attendance was generally limited to the critics and wealthy patrons.

Inventions of the twentieth century drastically reshaped the purpose and thrust of the popular arts. Radio made it possible for music to be aired, playscripts to be dramatized and heard, and sketches of comedic art to be broadcast. Motion pictures that could "talk" added another exciting and significant dimension. And, in a few short years, television projected art forms of all kinds—oral, aural, and visual—into myriad living rooms around the world. Concurrently, due to the invention of the phonograph, the public could experience over and over again the hearing of a chosen piece of music; and the refinements of tapes and cassettes facilitated the handling and the playing of an even broader and more personal selection of music and of recordings of great dramas and great speeches. Innovations to speed the processes of printing dramatically raised the output and allowed the intro-duction of the mass-produced paperback book. The same production break-throughs enabled small-circulation magazines to focus upon and specialize in single art forms. Because of these and other technological inventions, like the computer and the earth-circling communication satellite, millions of the world's exploding populations have been exposed to and significantly influenced by the persuasive power of the popular arts. In addition, the older forms of art and media have interacted and combined to produce ancillary effects which are, in fact, entirely new presentational forms. Elvis Presley performing on television is not Presley in "live" performance. A videotape can "telescope" time, rescheduling significant events and enter-tainment for maximum viewing at a more convenient moment. And consider what such technological innovations as slow-motion film, split screen, and instant playback have done to revolutionize and popularize athletic contests (which in turn help to sell beer, automobiles, razors, and shaving lotions).

Art as Persuasion

What makes art an effective instrument of persuasion is the viewer's unique perception of the artistic event as he experiences it. All audiences, when they are about to attend or experience an event—whether "live" or electronic—have certain expectations about the *content* of that event. When the event is a political rally, the audience anticipates discussion and exhortation. When the event is a concert—a Presley concert, for instance— the concert-goer would expect to hear, among other old favorites, "You Ain't Nothin' but a Hound Dog."

In addition to expectations regarding content, audiences also have

anticipations as to the *form* and *intent* of the presentation. The form
of a political rally is primarily a succession of public speeches, with
perhaps some preliminary and "transitional" music designed to attract
attention and add a pleasurable, but secondary, dimension. The political
spectator knows that, above all, the public-address form is designed to
maintain or change his attitudes and beliefs. He naturally, therefore, comes
to the event prepared for a verbal onslaught on his political attitudes; and
he sharpens his critical senses in order to analyze the ideological arguments
with which he knows he will be bombarded. He will be alert to anything
that accords with his views and can be applauded, and equally ready to
reject claims and assertions contrary or inimical to those views.

*If the popular arts have so much
persuasive potential, why aren't
they being exploited? Or are they?*

In contrast, the concert-goer, anticipating a full evening of music
intended solely for the purpose of providing esthetic enjoyment, does not
expect his attitudes to be challenged, his beliefs to be threatened. In music,
usually, he anticipates no persuasiveness as such; and so, of course, he does
not mentally brace himself to counter arguments or to refute ideas, even if
some were to be embedded or disguised in the song, the opera, or the
festival. Similarly, a poem often may be enjoyed for reasons other than its
ideological content; frequently it may be appreciated for such stylistic
elements as its rhythm, its imagery, the precision and compactness of its
phrasing, the delicacy of its structural balance, and for its power to evoke
mood and emotion. Generally speaking, those who read poetry do not
become argumentative about its substantive ideas or disqualify a poet's
work because of his political beliefs. Similarly, with regard to the lyrics of a
song, a listener can enjoy "Puff, the Magic Dragon" without buying into its
alleged exaltation of smoking marijuana; he can appreciate the music without
feeling prompted to debate the legalization of grass.

What is important to remember is that, although the auditor is appreci-
ating the poem or song for its literary or musical qualities, he is nevertheless
absorbing the *content*. Since he perceives the form as being pleasurable rather
than persuasive, he may listen to the piece many times. Thus, even though
the message may be subtle, the fact that it is repeated over and over—on radio,
television, stereo, and cassette—means that millions of people will hear it.
This repetition makes the potential power of the piece enormous. While
the Federal Communications Commission may limit the broadcast or televised speeches of political figures, it has not similarly restricted the singing
of Neil Young or the sarcastic comedy routines of Don Rickles. We may

quite correctly conclude, then, that when members of an audience witness
or experience an artistic performance, they often suspend judgment or make
no critical evaluation of the *persuasive* effect of the work.

Artistic License

That a viewer suspends or abrogates judgment of controversial content is an
acknowledged part of artistic license. There is an unstated assumption
between artist and audience that political or moral biases are to be discounted
to allow the artist freedom of creation or of expression. This assumption
would probably be subject to reexamination when applied to such an
obviously political play as *MacBird!* or to some of the more blatant revolutionary songs and poems. But generally the assumptions of artistic license
stand unchallenged. There are few rhetorical analyses of the revolutionary
strategies of Donovan. The fact of the matter is, however, that the strategies
are present—and virulent.

```
Rock music was born of a revolt against the sham of
Western culture:  It was direct and gutsy and spoke
to the senses.  As such it was profoundly subversive.
It still is.
                  --Jonathan Eisen, The Age of Rock¹
```

That the popular arts are considered essentially *entertainment* gives them
a decided advantage over other and more direct forms of verbal expression.
They are normally pleasurable, and at the same time they lower the receiver's
resistance to whatever subtle persuasion may be embedded in them. At a
distinct disadvantage in this respect are such directly communicative forms as
the lecture, the public address, and the personal encounter. Their direct
form proclaims their obvious intent. Even if these forms are intended to be
informative or inspirational in their impact, audiences do not view them as
entertainment. On the other hand, as we have noted, most of our music,
film, and nightclub routines are perceived almost entirely as pleasurable,
esthetic events utterly devoid of subtle or sinister "impurities" of persuasion
against which we must defend ourselves. The "lively" arts, being entertaining,
encourage us to attend and pay attention. We may eagerly buy a ticket to a
Joan Baez concert and listen entranced to her singing. But a lecture or a
public address is another matter. Unless we have a special or vested interest
in the subject or the sociopolitical stance of the speaker, we may be
reluctant to attend even if the event is admission free. If we do decide to go,
we start with a defensive frame of mind, anticipating that at best the
experience will be boring. Potentially, the speech—and certainly the lecture—
proffers more intellectual justification, but it is Baez' music which generates

repeated applause and quite frequently the audience's insistence upon an encore.

The so-called stand-up comedy act—whether staged in a nightclub or on television—illustrates even more strikingly the peculiar advantage of the entertainment form as a vehicle of persuasion. Many comedians induce audiences to laugh at political jokes even though these jokes reflect sentiments which the same audience would find objectionable in a speech or formal address.

```
I have to fly to Kansas City, Missouri, right after
the show.  This white cat moved into an all colored
neighborhood and some colored bigots burned a
watermelon on his lawn.
                        --Dick Gregory, comedian[2]
```

The late Lenny Bruce was famous for his blackly humorous attacks on sacred targets. People who laughed at his comedy routine about Eleanor Roosevelt's fabulous breasts probably would find the idea repulsive or at least offensive if Bruce had presented it in the form of a straight speech and without the shield of humor.* But given the nightclub/entertainment surroundings, most of the audience—even though they may have downgraded the comedian as being foul—tended to discount the grossness and to laugh. Using the format of comedic commentary, Bruce forced an alternate view of the dignified former First Lady upon them. By tossing his darts amid a mileu of liquor and laughter, the comedian was able to disguise his attack and achieve a tolerant audience reception.

Of course, the tactic of comedic commentary can backfire, especially if the target happens to be an extremely influential or powerful politician. Mort Sahl, who used humorous license to comment upon the foibles and fallacies of the presidency, regardless of the party which happened to be in power, purportedly found his contracts cancelled and the number of his engagements drastically curtailed after he tried to "take on" the Kennedy clan.

The Purity of Art Forms

Another factor which enables popular art forms to be unobtrusively but powerfully persuasive is the audience's perception of the "purity" of these forms. The artist is not considered the arch manipulator as is, for example, the public speaker. There have been too many lies and too many unfilled promises delivered in the form of speeches. As communication, public

---

*In his routine, which is reprinted in *The Essential Lenny Bruce*, ed. John Cohn (New York: Ballantine Books, 1970), p. 239, Bruce spoke about a friend of his who supposedly walked in on Mrs. Roosevelt while she was dressing.

speaking has been somewhat discredited. Because, in the public mind, artistic creativity is not as closely associated with business and politics as is public speaking, art forms are traditionally considered as rather unbiased and unsullied outlets of expression. You can trust a folksinger. When has a balladeer seriously extolled the virtues of General Motors?

As a people, however, we are becoming increasingly—and, perhaps, uneasily—aware that we cannot consistently perceive all art as being above manipulative intent. Many television programs which in themselves are highly artistic and unbiased nevertheless enjoy commercial sponsorship. It is not unusual for a too creative piece to be censored by a queasy company willing to sponsor only art that is consistent with its conception of an easily offended public. That, in fact, has come to be the prevailing practice, the essential economic fact of life for television. And in the films also we find some straightforward, unabashed propaganda. One example is *Battle of Algiers*, a how-to-do-it guide for revolution. Obviously, the appeal of this kind of film—and its employment of persuasion—is more direct than, say, an Ingmar Bergman film, which is often vague and mystical. *Algiers* assaults the spectator with violent action and patriotic speeches; Bergman's *Wild Strawberries*, through its mood and pacing, works more subtly on the viewer. However, even if we use the extreme example of *Battle of Algiers*, our initial assertion is still valid: the filmic format makes its theme more acceptable to far larger groups than would be the same theme expressed in a public speech.

Music as Persuasion

Repeatedly in the preceding pages of this chapter we have touched briefly upon the prevalence, pervasiveness, and persuasiveness of music as an art form. And in the two chapters following this one, we will explore at least two major facets of the form more fully. At this point, however, before concluding this overview, we should note in particular a few of the reasons why popular music is potentially one of the most persuasive of all of the arts. Clearly, its advantages in this respect are unique and varied: (1) Thematically, modern popular music is relatively simple. When it is coupled with the insistent repetitiveness of today's rock lyrics, listeners need exert very little effort to grasp the ideas, persuasive or otherwise, that the song is trying to communicate. (2) Even more important, perhaps, is the fact that the listeners themselves—thanks to the easy availability and relatively low cost of records, record-players, and cassettes—can play the same song over and over, scores or even hundreds of times. Not beyond belief is the estimate that an admirer of Bob Dylan's music may play his "Blowin' in the Wind" fifty times in a single evening. In contrast, very few people will play a recording of a speech, much less purchase a recording of one. Consider, then, how much greater are the opportunities for the singer of popular songs to make repeated and persuasive impressions upon a listener. (3) Since an infectious beat or a simple lyric has a way of embedding itself in our conscious and subconscious minds, the subliminal persuasiveness of the song is always with us. Once our thinking has been impregnated with the idea, we multiply its effect manyfold and perpetuate it within ourselves—and by ourselves.

Would it make sense for a teacher to write his lecture in poetry or rock lyrics?

In total effect, while as yet there may be no scientific proof that popular music can influence conversions to ideas, political and cultural, it dins into our ears so constantly and bombards our minds so heavily that the possibility of such influencing cannot be shrugged off. Nor can we dismiss an even stronger possibility that repeated playings of music and lyrics *when coupled with more direct forms of persuasion*—a political speech, for example—will produce significant attitude change.

Two thousand college students riot after hearing attorney William Kunstler discuss the Conspiracy Trial of the Chicago Seven.

Question: What caused the riot?
   Kunstler's speech?
   The trial?
   Society?
   Bob Dylan?
   Rolling Stone?
   All of the above?

That a single speech by a middle-aged militant or that any other similar communicative event can in and by itself produce mass conversion to an idea is both implausible and improbable. What is much more likely is that a *combination* and *repetition* of speechmaking, popular music, comedic acts and commentary, and "guerrilla" movies have *all* contributed to the attitudinal shifts which are taking place in our society. Kunstler's speech may have sparked what *appeared* to be riot-oriented conversion, but years of "softening up" by Phil Ochs, the Beatles, the comic strips of R. Crump, and polemic films like *Algiers* and *Z* made it possible.

Significantly, the popular arts have not been in the hands of the Establishment (a condition which prevailed in earlier eras). If anything, the rock musician, the stand-up comedian, or the modern poet is an outsider who attacks Society's conventions. Since the marriage of the popular arts with the mass media, much of America—much of the world, in fact—has been steadily exposed to alternate life styles. In matters of civil rights, Vietnam, and ecology, for example, the popular arts have exerted steady pressure on a number of major governmental policies during the past decade. There are few folk songs defending the notion of racial or economic inferiority, and very few poems glorifying the backlash. These negativistic, reactionary stances rarely are taken by musicians, poets, and other artists. And this may very well be an important reason why the popular arts remain highly articulate antagonists of twentieth-century bias and bigotry.

Allan Ginsberg's poem "Howl" makes it into most contemporary anthologies.

***Portnoy's Complaint* convinced many Christians that Jewish fathers are constipated.**

The Beatles sold more guitars than any advertiser ever dreamed possible.

8 Ritual and Music: The Blues

Rhetorically as well as musically, the revival of blues music in America is significant. Blues, when sung well, communicates. Its power can cut across barriers of time and space to reach anyone who has suffered. Blues can be persuasive, profound, and deeply moving. When, for example, bluesman Muddy Waters shouts the lyrics about his "no-good woman" over the driving beat of his rhythm section, every man—regardless of his musical taste—must be stirred by Muddy's emotion and power. The purpose of this chapter is to examine the blues as an indirect, but one of the earliest, means of social persuasion and dissent.

The rhetoric of the blues originated in the spirituals and field hollers of the black slave in the South. The music that grew from these sources is distinct in character, and in it we can detect numerous implications of ways in which music can affect attitudes. Although there are many variations of the blues, ranging from the unamplified steel guitars of the Mississippi Delta bluesmen to the loud, amplified renditions of the urban bluesmen found in Northern ghettos, all of them share certain characteristics. These characteristics will serve as the focus of this analysis. It should be noted in passing that "soul" music, although an offshoot of the blues, adds gospel chord patterns and certain jazz orchestrations which deviate sufficiently from blues to exclude it from the present discussion.*

What is blues? One way of describing blues is to call it an oral history of the blacks, not of all blacks, but of the field slaves, who originated blues—devil songs—from a background that black writer Richard Wright called "that confounding triptych of the convict, the migrant, the rambler, the steel driver, the ditch digger, the roustabout, the pimp, the prostitute, the urban or rural outsider."[1] The bluesman sings about his personal problems, of love—won, lost, or forgotten—of jealousy, of disappointment, and of men and women cruelly crushed by the brutalizing forces of hunger, hopeless impoverishment, and agonizing despair implicit in the conditions in which they are compelled to exist.

The blues is a constant reminder to blacks of their past, a past both glorious and sad. To blues bars and clubs all over the rural South and urban North it brings the sound of black history, creating an experience closer to religion and ritual than to the secular and entertainment. As a child listening to blues-artist Bessie Smith, jazz singer Billie Holiday recalled that "sometimes the record would make me so sad I'd cry up a storm. Other times the same damn record would make me so happy I'd forget about how much hard-earned money the session in the parlour was costing me."[†] It was the same Bessie Smith whose records reconciled black writer James Baldwin, while in Switzerland, to being a black man in America.

The bluesmen left behind not only an oral history, but also a distillation of the way many blacks in the ghettos of the North and the South felt, and still feel, about the remnants of life permitted them by "the man" downtown:

In the wee midnight hours, long 'fore the break of day,
In the wee midnight hours, long 'fore the break of day,
When the blues creep upon you and carry your mind away . . .

—Leroy Carr, "Midnight Hour Blues"[2]

---

*Examples of primarily soul singers are Dionne Warwick, Bo Diddley, Chuck Berry, and Aretha Franklin. Among well-known blues singers are John Lee Hooker, Buddy Guy, J. B. Hutto, Junior Wells, and Sonny Terry.

†Billie Holiday with William Dufty, *Lady Sings the Blues* (New York: Lancer, 1965), p. 11. Miss Holiday ran errands for a house of prostitution, and in return listened to the management's blues records.

The typical blues singer delivers a line of lyrics echoed by an instrumental bridge to the second line, which is similar or identical to the first line. Each sung or spoken phrase in a blues lyric is followed by a complementary instrumental response:

Blues jumped a rabbit,
Run him one solid mile.
(instrumental response)
Blues jumped a rabbit,
Run him one solid mile.
(instrumental response)

The thought begun in the first two lines is somehow resolved in the rhyming third line:

The rabbit fell down,
Cryin' like a natural child.

—Blind Lemon Jefferson, "Rabbit Foot Blues"[3]

The instrumental response is essential to the structure of blues, reinforcing and balancing the verbal phrase it follows. In blues, the musical response is as important to the composition as the lyrics. A great bluesman perfectly integrates the singing style and lyrics with a complementary instrumental style. In blues, the instrument is as important as the voice. Ideally, the instrument acts as an extension of the bluesman's experience, whether joyous or sorrowful. This combination of singing and instrumental break is known as "call and response" and is the essence of blues. For example, the late Sonny Boy Williamson echoed his lyrics in the song "Help Me" by combining his wailing harmonica with a rhythmic organ. In this piece, Sonny Boy plays blues by uniting the lyrics and the music to create a mood of despair and loneliness. Undercutting the blues mood are the sounds of Sonny's harmonica and the rhythm of the organ—evidence that, despite his blues, Sonny Boy still copes. It is through the interplay of the lyrics, music, and sound that the irony of blues is illustrated. Sonny Boy is able to overcome his blues only by playing them. It is this dialogue created by the "call and response" which makes blues blues, and identifies blues as a distinctive communicative art.

The blues lyrics themselves are conversational and terse. There are few connectives, and the vocabulary is plain, with few embellishments. Blues critics agree that blues lyrics are frequently composed spontaneously and without the usual Tin Pan Alley cleanup. The lyrics often flow like a stream of consciousness rather than a carefully planned, well-balanced piece of

music. When the composer is right, his lyrics have a naturalness and direct-
ness, unlike much popular music.

In the evenin', baby, when the sun go down,
In the evenin', mama, when the sun go down,
Well, it's hard to tell, it's hard to tell, oh baby,
After the sun go down, an' the sun go down.
                        —Guitar (Robert) Welch, "When the Sun Go Down"[4]

The meaning of much of blues lyrics is often couched in double meanings. The precursors of the blues, field hollers and work songs, often doubled
as codes that allowed slaves to communicate plans for rebellion or their
hatred and scorn for their overseers. Or the music acted just to warm them
with the knowledge that they had something of their own, if only a language,
that the whites could not control. Later, after the Civil War, the developing
blues songs used double meanings, as did much of the language that blacks
began to develop among themselves.

While blues lyrics are distinctive, they make blues only in concert with
the music. The blues usually has twelve bars, though this can be varied to
eight, sixteen, or any other multiple of four. It is usually in 4/4 time, but it
can be fitted to other rhythm patterns as well. There is a blues chromaticism,
or blues scale, which has African origins and which differs from the Western
European scale. In order to play the correct blues notes, it is necessary to
bend or flatten certain notes. The flattening gives blues that characteristic
raw, deep, earthy tone which combines with lyrics to make a distinctive folk
music identifiable.

When performed to predominantly black audiences, blues is fundamen-
tally a ceremonial rhetoric. The recitation of the blues is a wistful reaffirma-
tion of basic values. It is not unlike a Fourth of July oration or a eulogy for
a fallen leader. The combination of blues notes and lyrics represents a
common set of symbols that is the language creation of an entire people.
Blues, like much ceremonial rhetoric, reinforces a sense of community and
identity. Black playwright LeRoi Jones claims: "The blues impulse was a
psychological correlative that obscured the most extreme ideas of assimilation
for most Negroes, and made any notion of the complete abandonment of the
traditional black culture an unrealizable possibility."[5] Mixed with the
affirmation of values is a nostalgia for the South that seems undeserved. But
one can be nostalgic and still not wish to return.

The ceremonial function of blues accounts for much of black upset with
white blues singers. For a white to sing blues is like Perry Como singing the
Yom Kippur liturgy "Kol Nidre," or Fidel Castro delivering a Fourth of
July oration. It is not just mediocre, but profane. Blues is a music that not
only fulfills a need for blacks, but is also their personal property.

Living Is Trouble. To play the blues, Johnny had to go to the black clubs. "In those days, I didn't get any resentment because I was white," he says. "They knew I wasn't putting on and that I loved the music and I could play it as good as they could. It was great." Today, he is puzzled by the notion that only Negroes have suffered enough to sing the blues. "I've had trouble too, and everybody has trouble. Just living is a different kind of trouble." Living for Johnny meant dealing with a minority problem of his own: "Being an albino is hard, and when you're younger, it's a lot harder. When they said 'Hey, Whitey,' it was just like calling someone a nigger. They called me anything—fag, queer, freak."
—Johnny Winter, blues singer[6]

In the same sense, listening to the blues may be a necessity for some blacks—like church attendance for some Catholics on Easter Sunday. One does not choose to go—one has to go. Some rituals—that on the surface may appear frivolous—recharge men's souls. It is difficult to imagine a guy with a girl on his arm, a beer in his hand, listening as a worshiper to raw, rough, visceral blues lyrics. But who defines the nature of the worship house? When the bluesman starts confessing his misery and the congregation hears the truth, the difference in structure of the temple is unimportant.

Heard somebody knocking, wondered who it could be,
Heard somebody knocking, wondered who it could be,
Nobody but the mailman bringing me misery.
—Nick Nicholls, "Riverside Blues"[7]

One of the most striking aspects of blues is the strong emphasis upon confession in the bluesman's performance. Although the bluesman is usually interested in his own self, he describes common problems that can be easily shared by black audiences. He is—on stage—the culmination of the black man's experiences.

You don't know, you don't know, you don't know, doggone you,
You don't know, you don't know, my min',
But when you sees me laughin', that's just to keep from cryin'.
—Herman E. Johnson, "You Don't Know My Min'"[8]

Lyrics like these are the sentiments of countless thousands of his fellows. When the blues singer tells of mistreatment in a love affair, or of job discrimination, he knows that other blues singers and other audiences in other towns may be feeling the same problems.

To heighten the drama of the blues ritual, the performer often uses a number of devices that are reminiscent of fundamentalist preachers. Frequently, bluesmen will stutter or seem to stumble hopelessly over a number of simple words. The momentary breakdown indicates the sincerity of the singer, implying no façade and an honest performance. Some bluesmen use nonverbal communication to indicate stresses and joys. Brushing away tears or falling to the knees punctuate sad moments and reinforce sincerity. Cry singer James Brown, who sometimes sings blues, often falls to his knees and, apparently crying, asks, "Did you eveh cry?" Some bluesmen scream, groan, lie on their backs, and kick their feet in the air, as well as doing some bumps and grinds. All these gymnastics are part of the power and intensity of the blues performance.

Black audiences respond to the blues confession with sympathy and empathy. Audiences interact with "yeah" or "Tell it like it is," not only because they understand and appreciate, but because they, too, are immersed in the confession. It is traditional in blues that the audience feels no sense of alienation from the singer. The bluesman and his audience are one. This relationship is in marked contrast to the traditional stage situation in which the audience clearly is separated from the performer. This sense of oneness and participation in the blues, coupled with its historical significance, can make for highly effective communication. As Charles Keil writes:

A good blues lyric is a representative anecdote, the distillation of a problem, the naming of a malaise. Today, a good rendering of an urban blues lyric is also a representative antidote, ritually acted out, for the malady named. The naming--and--curing ceremony is a grand synecdote (literally--from the Greek--"a receiving together"), and this dramatized figure of speech is effective to the degree that the man stands for his people, the people for their man--one for all, and all for one.[9]

Extending the Keil analogy, we have in blues a therapeutic rhetoric. Those who enter fully into the blues ritual (performer or listener) are potentially transformed or cured through the naming ceremony. The public naming of the malaise is evident: on Passover, Jews still recite the ten plagues of ancient Israel:

Blood	Boils
Frogs	Hail
Gnats	Locusts
Flies	Darkness
Murrain	Slaying of the First-Born

In early fall, football coaches still recite the injuries and misfortunes of their "immature" ball club to batteries of sports writers who have been hearing the same story for years:

| Hamstring | Concussion |
| Twisted Knee | Sprain |

There is something regular and satisfying about the naming of the malaise for most of us. The group-naming process is apparently psychologically rewarding, and sometimes healing. That therapy is a central characteristic of blues should not be surprising, since the music is drawn from the experiences of the people it now serves and regenerates.

```
The blues is, you know, a feelin'.  You got to feel
it to play it.  It's not even--it's unwriteable,
man.  I mean, I've tried to get somebody to arrange
some of the things I was playin' because I got some
kids wanted me to teach 'em.  Well, I say, "If you
can read it, I can write it," you know, so I go in
to arrange it and writer there told me, said, "Man,
I can't write that.  Tha's impossible."  So, I mean,
then you know you definitely have to feel this to
play.  I mean you just have to hear what I'm playin'
and just keep it in your mind and play.
                    --Buddy Guy, blues singer[10]
```

The blues is a unique rhetorical transaction complete with its own language, rhythms, and rituals. Its power comes from a long history of shared language and value conventions that are unique to a certain minority who produced the blues during years of deprivation and struggle. Blues is nativistic in that its presence is a reminder to blacks, and other creators of blues, that a person cannot totally abandon his culture. In this sense, blues is a closed discourse—open only to those who share the symbols.

9 Keeping in Touch: AM Rock Radio

More hits . . . more of them.
Boss Radio, thanking you for making
us the Sound of the Southland.

The medium of "the kids" is rock-music radio. It is not that youth in any way control what goes over rock radio, but that rock radio is aimed exclusively at them, to the exclusion of their parents, uncles, aunts, or anyone else out there over thirty. Whether it is the "Top Ten," "Boss 30," "Golden 40," or "The Big 89 with hits back to back on WLS," the radio defines what rock music is. This definition is so complete that for something to be rock music it has to be radio-played or a radio-played derivative.

A piece of rock music cannot become known unless it is played over rock radio because neither exposure in a rock magazine like *Rolling Stone* nor a mass distribution in the record stores will interest enough people to make the record a hit. In fact, a manufacturer's survey of rock sales found that over 80 percent of albums are purchased because people have heard a particular portion—one or two of the songs—over the radio and liked them. If a disc jockey does not play a piece of music, it cannot survive and cannot be considered a living part of rock.

SEED: What's done in terms of promoting a record?

MAX: To begin with, the record manufacturer sends the distributor promo material—photographs and album samples. It's assumed that the promo man listens to a record and promotes it accordingly. The promo man also introduces a record to D.J.'s and tries to get air-play. This means approaching the program director at the top 40 stations. He selects the music to be played and changes it weekly. The object of much of the promo man's work is to get a record breaking in several areas, and then say "This record is a winner—it's number 32 on WIXY, etc." It's really murder to come in with a new record and a new artist to a top 40 or format station. Unless it happens to be a killer record. Most of record promotion is personal contacts. Even the record company's other-than-promotion executives keep in close contact with the D.J.'s and the media. That's why some of the companies are more successful than others. When I was with Chess [Record Company], I would often be called in to talk with a D.J. to ask to get a record played. It all adds up to how heavy the record is and, secondly, as to how heavy the promotion man is.

—Chicago Seed interview[1]

The definition of rock used in this chapter is obviously very broad and makes rock identical to popular music. There are rock experts who would distinguish rock by the various sounds of different movements and groups. However, this classification isn't really practical, for rock's sound is always changing, and includes folk, folk rock, acid rock, hard rock, blues, and a number of other music classifications.

With a wide-ranging eclecticism, popular music has adapted to itself a bewildering variety of musical traditions and instruments from the classic Indian sitar to the most recent electronic synthesizers favored by composers of "serious" concert music.

--Robert Rosenstone, "The Times They Are A-Changin'"[2]

Regardless of the musical classification, much of the music sounds alike when broadcast over rock radio. Most AM radios, unlike stereos, have poor reproduction; and the music subtleties are camouflaged by static. The owners of rock-radio stations know that much of their product is received over low-quality, eight-transistor, $8.95 Specials that gasp and squeak from inferior craftsmanship and weak batteries. The poor sound is worsened by overcrowding on the dial, which pulls stations into sonic overlap with one another. Thus, the modern rock-radio strategist keys his music content to that which can best be heard when heard poorly. This means that frequently played rock music is often simple. These songs have a strong beat and usually have one good, catchy riff that is repeated often, such as the early Beatles' hits and songs like "Indiana Wants Me."* Most of the quality rock is played over FM, where the sound is better, the pace slower, and D.J.s free to choose a wider range of selections.† Above all, however, rock is tied to what AM radio plays and defines as rock music.

Rock radio also determines for its listeners what they are going to hear—and makes them want to hear it. The owners of rock radio discovered, in one of their countless audience surveys, that the typical listener tunes in for an average of only twenty minutes. To complicate matters, a survey of 6000 Los Angeles kids by Bill Drake, the most successful of the rock-radio owners, revealed that 47 percent of kids tune out because a bad record is being played.[3] As a result, the radio people are playing fewer records and playing them more often, so that listeners will become familiar with a select list of records, which they will be less likely to tune out. This strategy is called "a tight playlist," and it means that out of the 300 or 400 records released each week only a few new ones are going to surface for that period. For a Drake station, this means anywhere from three to six new records per week, and for the average rock station, between five and ten records. According to the "top forty" reasoning, which is based on the kids' listening habits, if a record is twelfth, it is better than a record that is forty-third, both in number of record sales and in quality. "Top forty" reasoning means that listeners are not exposed to a wide variety of rock music from which they can select their favorite. The Bill Drakes determine what will make the "top forty" by deciding what records they will introduce.

The phenomenon of the rock-music medium is complex. The music itself is only a portion of the rock-radio experience, as rock radio provides the listener with the correct time, "current" music, weather, and news. The medium of rock radio is not giving youth the music *they* choose, since much

---

*For a discussion of what makes quality rock, see Ned Rorem, "The Music of the Beatles," in *The Age of Rock*, ed. Jonathan Eisen (New York: Random House, Inc., 1969), pp. 149-159. Also see "Lennon's Song: The Man Can't F**k Our Music," by Ben Fong-Torres, in *Rolling Stone:* 76 (February 18, 1971), pp. 1, 6.

†There is increasing evidence that these factors are beginning to erode the supremacy of AM radio. The Pulse, Inc., radio ratings for Chicago, as reported in *The Chicago Daily News*, March 5, 1971, p. 59, indicated a strong upsurge in listenership for the newer "underground radio" stations and a decline for AM stations.

of rock radio plays songs that are technically inferior, even if they are among the "golden harvest of top hits." But the music, incorporated into the general flow of the sound of rock radio, is only the *apparent* reason for listening. The *actual* reason is more sweeping and basic.

Many rock-radio listeners tune in for the progression of human existence. In presenting clock time, weather, news, and music, D.J.s are plugging their listeners into the events that are constantly reshaping their lives. All the information on rock radio is presented as a continuous flow of the same kind of sound. D.J.s present the time and news with the same rhythm and timing that makes them sound like part of an introduction to the next record.

```
The UN today asked for release of two Algerians
held by Israel. . . . It's 3:15, KHJ Kahuna Cockatoo
time. . . . The weather is 79, cloudy, clear, and
h-e-e-r-e is Creedence Clearwater Revival . . . with
"Lookin' Out My Back Door" . . .
```

Rock radio, whether reciting weather or news, is really part of the same experience. The sound is a fast-paced bombardment which conveys to the listener the ever-increasing cacophony of modern existence. The voice of the D.J. is that of ever-moving, never-hesitating mankind, blowing up with information and always on the verge of explosion.

The sound of rock radio is so frantic that few people listen very closely. Most people listen to rock radio while doing something else. They tune in while studying, working on the car, loving, or doing a lot of other activities. If people really concentrated on the shrill, high-impact presentation of rock radio, many would become neurotic. Half listening, however, allows one to tune in to the flow of existence without surrendering time devoted to a useful project.

What keeps the entire rock-radio operation on edge is the competition to be number one in ratings. Being a disc jockey is a high-pressure existence, for he knows that failure to hold listeners for his station will put him out on the street or, worse, back in the sticks. This D.J. anxiety is part of the sound, and it makes a perfect metaphor for keeping in touch with the flow. The D.J.'s existence is tight; so is the state of the world. When he is on the air, he is going flat out to cope with pressure and tension in his own life, and this is one real sound of the seventies.

The actual content of the rock-radio program also contributes to the idea of progress, or to the flow of life. The theme of rock radio is staying in touch. Announcing the time, of course, defines progress. When it is 8:41, we know we can anticipate that we will be informed when it is 8:52. In this way, the listener can measure the intervals of time being ticked off. The weather also is a sign that our condition is ever changing. The fact that

"Berlin is CLOUD-EEE and RAIN-EEE," and that "Tallll-ahh-haaasseeee is a WON-der-ful SEVENTEE-TWOO" tells listeners the condition of the world's weather, one dimension of the world's condition.

For most of us, there is a strong faith that what is on the newscast is what the world is doing. In trying to keep in touch, most listeners are appreciative of the people out there who sift the information. We know there is too much happening out there, and we want the most important events highlighted for our attention. Rock radio gives us the news in a brief, fast-paced, staccato, every-thirty-minutes summary, so we do not lose the flow. Yet, it does not burden or bore listeners with details, because in another half an hour the world will be somewhere else and all we want to do is to keep in touch.

The rock music is the most important factor in maintaining the continuous flow. In the music, we can see the changing of our own tastes, of ourselves, and all the other people we assume are listening—and changing with us. We hear individual songs introduced, become hits, gradually fade—and then hear the cycle renewed. When a "Golden Hit of Yesteryear" is revived for the week, we are made wistfully aware of the passage of time. Throughout the years of listening to rock radio, we can measure progress by the changes in music. The Grateful Dead start playing country; Little Richard comes back; The Who slip into the Top Ten; and the Cream and Moby Grape split. As Alvin Toffler puts it:

Change is avalanching down upon our heads, and most people are utterly unprepared to cope with it.[4]

Rock radio tunes its listeners into their very own existence. The flow of life today can only be captured by a medium like rock radio which has the technological apparatus—teletypes, transmitters, etc.—to plug us into the overwhelming pace of Toffler's avalanche: "What's going on in the Near East?" "Did the Jets win today?" "Is it raining in Moscow?" "Crack up on Highway 49?" "What're the Beatles into?" It is true that music is the overt reason for listening to rock radio—initially. But the time, news, and weather are there because of what they do to our concept of the music. They help identify the music with a direction we can give our lives—even if it means slicked down hair.

What makes AM rock radio commercially manipulative is that its dependence on the flow also creates dependence on the products advertised. The flow that provides the listeners with time, weather, news, and music is merely a strategy for the selling of skin creams, eye makeup, and pimple removers. D.J.s naturally integrate hair cream into the flow. The better the flow, the higher the ratings—the higher the ratings, the more sponsors—the more sponsors, the richer the stations.

That AM rock radio is enduring can be seen in the number of thirty-year-olds who still listen. While many teen-agers "grow out of" rock, there is increasing evidence that rock radio has become a way of life for some people. It is to this older audience that rock radio dedicates its "Solid Gold Weekend" or "Oldies—But Goodies" features:

SUGAR SHACK
ROCK AROUND THE CLOCK
HEY, JUDE
YOU SEND ME
BLUEBERRY HILL
CHANTILLY LACE

If you want *good* rock, listen to FM or buy a phonograph. The Bill Drakes will not suffer if you grow old or go underground, because rock radio will produce a new audience with each new junior-high-school class.

ROCK RADIO IS NOT MUSIC, BUT A FLOW.

ROCK RADIO IS SEXLESS; LIVE ROCK IS SEX.

ACNE IS A ROCK-RADIO PUT-ON.

10 The Rhetoric of Film

MOVIES: JUJYFRUITS AND JOHN WAYNE

Potentially, there are few media more persuasive than film. As the viewer sits in a darkened theater, at stillpoint, all the action is brought to him. The only obvious light in the theater is reflected from the screen. Because all movement occurs within the confines of that screen and is brought as effortlessly as possible to his attention, a spectator does not have to exert as much concentration as he would if he were watching a play or reading a novel. In a Western, a stagecoach chase can involve thousands of Indians, a road under construction, trick shooting, and stuntmen. Yet, through the illusion of the film—the way it is photographed, cut, and edited—the viewer is spared all of the detail work.

The first part of this chapter will examine how Hollywood used the mirage of the movies to influence and shape the consciences of the American civilian and soldier during World War II. The second section will contrast the war-film persuasion with the new strategies of the contemporary film-maker.

The decade of the forties was the Age of the War Film. Having exploited fully the melodramatics of gangsterdom and having mined the drawing-room comedy to exhaustion, Hollywood turned eagerly to the interplay of men at war. The movie-makers of the Fighting Forties were dominated by large studios like Columbia, Warner Brothers, and Metro-Goldwyn-Mayer; and they cranked out pictures at the rate of one a week, fifty weeks a year. These studios converted to war with the same swiftness as did General Motors, International Harvester, and General Electric. While those manufacturers converted from automobiles, tractors, and radios to guns, planes, and radar, Hollywood's movie-makers changed their story lines, grabbed the cigar and gangster moll away from Edward G. Robinson, and jammed him into a major's uniform. When Hollywood went to war, it went with a vengeance; in fact, it created its own war.

A "Shooting" Script for the War

The typical war film burst with patriotism, and painted the hero's adversaries as something less than animals. Underlying each such movie were a number of presuppositions, and these were understood, accepted, and—usually—anticipated by the audience even before the credits flashed on the screen: The dirty Japs are short, big-toothed, little fellows with shifty eyes, who control an island in the Pacific. They torture people, rape fair-haired women, have eating and sex orgies after hours, and never give their prisoners any nourishment other than lice-infested rice and typhoid-ridden water. Sessue Hayakawa plays the sadistic officer who beats prisoners unmercifully. He had attended UCLA in 1937, where he starred in football and learned to speak English. He will take his own life when his troops are beaten by the more courageous American forces.

The film opens in the Marine Training Center in San Diego. There are the usual troubles in getting the new trainees together. The sergeant in charge of raw recruits is played by John Wayne or Robert Taylor or Gregory Peck or Clark Gable. He is tough, unrelenting, handsome, and seemingly maniacal about getting his men into shape. Often the sergeant is unmarried or divorced or a soldier of fortune. The "Kid," played by Van Johnson or Dane Clark or John Payne, is from Southern California, is in love, and lies in bed daydreaming about his boyhood sweetheart. He played high-school football (star halfback), jerked sodas, loved cars, and has a cute kid sister and wonderful, understanding parents who are more than willing to sacrifice their son to the war effort. Usually there is a final leave before the soldiers ship out, and the kid spends it shooting baskets with little brother, gabbing with the corner druggist, and necking with his girl in his dad's car. She promises to wait.

The men in the training platoon are a mixed lot: *Goldberg the Jew* from Brooklyn is soft-spoken, reads a lot, and would like to be a teacher or a writer. He is suspected of being a coward; but eventually—armed as a human time bomb—he will save the pinned-down company by single-handedly attacking a Jap machine-gun nest. Goldberg dies tragically—he always dies— and his death reminds the bigoted members of the platoon of how well a Jew can fight.

Kluzewski the Pole from Pittsburgh is the strong but stupid member of the group. He carries the submachine gun. He will save John Wayne in a dramatic moment by picking up two Japs and squashing their heads together. At the end of the movie, it is understood, he will return to his fat wife and three kids, and stoke steel furnaces for the rest of his life.

Juarez the Mexican from Arizona is thought by everyone to be a dirty thief. Early in the picture he is accused of stealing a hunting knife from the locker of Hanson the Swede. Juarez never is fully exonerated; but when the battle heats, he proves his courage and honesty by staying on the walkie-talkie amidst tremendous enemy fire, thereby engineering the saving of countless lives. Under lethal crossfire, only moments before he is to be killed, he explains to Kluzewski that there is nothing in Arizona for him to return to, and a few moments later he gets the final bullet. Such foreshadow-ing heightens the dramatic impact of most filmic deaths.

The Negro, who is nameless, doesn't say much, but he smiles a lot. He seems to understand orders, but never gives them. He is a minor character.

The Priest, or Pop, is Pat O'Brien or James Craig playing the wise, gentle chaplain. His purpose is to give perspective and narration to events. In talks with Sergeant Wayne/Taylor/Peck/Gable, he discusses the religious rightness of the American cause and the personal problems of the men. He also acts as a sounding board for military strategy. It is understood that he will escort the casketed bodies of Goldberg and Juarez to their respective home towns.

The Chicken Captain was in the National Guard. The town banker, he will find courage, usually when someone else dies for his cowardice. Walter Pidgeon or Ward Bond is a likely selection for this role.

Somehow—through adversity, comradeship, and the strain of battle—this motley crew of ethnic types transcend their differences and weld themselves into a potent fighting force. They kill thousands of Japanese; every time they pull a trigger—BLAM!—another son of Nippon plummets to the ground, his rifle spinning heavenward. But the enemy numbers ultimately overwhelm the Yanks, and their ranks are reduced to three brave souls manning a lone machine gun amidst thousands of onrushing foes. They fight doggedly and desperately on, despite shrewd enemy psychology voiced by an English-speaking Japanese who harangues them with propaganda.

```
Hey, Yank . . . the Dodgers beat the Cards 5 to 2
last night in Brooklyn.
```

```
Save me . . . save me . . . I'm hit . . . I'm
American.
```

Wave after wave of oriental fanatics finally kill one American, leaving only the badly wounded Pole and Sergeant Wayne/Taylor/Gable/Peck to fight. Finally, the sergeant, punchy from fatigue, picks up the machine gun; and while "America the Beautiful" is played in the background, he wipes out 150 dirty Japs.

```
WAKE ISLAND--CORREGIDOR--BATAAN--SALUTE TO THE
MARINES--GUADALCANAL DIARY--OBJECTIVE TOKYO--THEY
WERE EXPENDABLE--GUNG HO
```

The strategy of this type of film was to present the training group and their gradual welding into a potent, self-sacrificing force as a metaphor for citizen conduct in time of crisis. If the men in San Diego—having such diverse backgrounds and being alleged representatives of American ethnic groups—can become one, then the Jewish butcher, the Polish steel worker, and the Swedish farmer also can pull together to save gasoline, manufacture bombsights, grow more wheat, and write letters to lonely servicemen. The movie-makers—and the viewers—did not care that the films presented stereotypes with little reference to reality; critical judgment was subjugated in behalf of the war effort. The war movie thus had an appreciative audience of citizens who—between bites of Mason Dots, swigs of Coke, puffs of Lucky Strikes, and slurps of Holloway all-day suckers—burst into applause whenever American soldiers successfully attacked and bullet-slugged Japs spun bizarrely in death or flew grotesquely into the air.

This was Hollywood's portrayal of America at its best. A group of suspicious young American military recruits learn through hardships that there is one Mexican who does not steal and is brave. Why wasn't the Mexican ever the sergeant?

```
Hollywood, with its mass appeal through movies and
TV, has been a powerful force in maintaining stereo-
types.  Chinese are cooks or houseboys; Japanese are
spies; Mexicans are banditos; Negroes are clowns--
all of these stereotypes have appeared in countless
movies.  And most important, these have been the
only visible images of such groups as viewed by
millions of Americans.
     --Roger Daniels and Harry Kitano, American Racism[1]
```

What produced the sameness, and the rather tepid product, of the World War II film was the control by the heads of the Hollywood studios. Their financial resources and superior technical facilities offered advantages that produced a smooth product. Yet, according to movie critic Parker Tyler,[2] there were three unfortunate by-products of the big studio domination:

1. A lack of individual control in the movie-making process. The big studio bosses (Harry Cohn, Jack Warner, Louis Mayer) kept a tight control over the production and direction of their films. At Columbia, for example, most films were the product of Cohn's personal values, tastes, and artistic judgment. This meant that a script which ran counter to accepted mores was either rejected or doctored. The standard of living enjoyed by the blonde "kid" from Southern California and his family was a fabrication of American life which the studio heads promulgated through their films to millions of Americans.

2. The Hollywood system had little respect for original work. The system was based upon a formula picture which minimized risks by repeating the familiar. Hollywood remade the same movie countless times, varying only the details, the setting, and the cast:

```
BOY MEETS GIRL--
   THEY FALL IN LOVE--
      BREAK UP--
         MAKE UP.


TOUGH KID FROM NEW YORK SLUMS
   FIGHTS HIS WAY UP THE GANG LADDER--
      MEETS BEAUTIFUL GIRL--
         LIVES HIGH--
            GETS KILLED.
```

The business of Hollywood could not afford to take financial risks on unproven merchandise. If a studio produced a loser, it meant lower earning reports for stockholders and a general slowdown of the manufacturing process.

3. There was an unabashed desire to give the public what it seemed to want. Hollywood seldom risked striking out into new areas of controversy. If the public seemed to hesitate over Hollywood's taste, there were public relations men who worked on the recalcitrants.

An illustration of the astuteness of Tyler's criticism can be observed by examining *A Walk in the Sun*, certainly one of the best products of the Hollywood system. This film, directed by Lewis Milestone and starring Dana Andrews and Richard Conte, concerns soldiers in Sicily who, during lulls in battle, philosophize about life, death, and fate. What distinguishes the film is the honesty of the soldiers' performances as they strain to communicate with one another under the stress of battle.

As Tyler notes, the chief strategy of *A Walk in the Sun* is one which underlies most film soldiers' thinking:

```
As the byword in the platoon goes:  "It's a stinking
situation."  Yet there is nothing to do but get
out of it as quickly as possible.  The path by which
to do this is naturally to obey orders--to defeat
the enemy rather than capitulate to him.³
```

The strategy is not ambiguous and needs little interpretation for the movie-goer. The solution of fighting one's way out of adversity had been reinforced in Hollywood's earlier war films so that it seemed the only alternative. Actually, however, there are other strategies the soldiers could have executed to extract themselves from the "stinking war" and still not violate the value judgment that war is a miserable, unpleasant experience:

HIDE OUT UNTIL THE BATTLE ABATES.
SURRENDER TO THE ENEMY.
COMMIT SUICIDE.
GO AWOL.

For the Hollywood of the forties, these strategies did not surface because the studios valued their relationship with the Armed Services, and the highly centralized studio operation was not to be placed in jeopardy. While *A Walk in the Sun* was a fine, sensitive film which illustrated film-studio Hollywood at its best, it was not a great film because it reflected a serious limitation of alternatives. Its art was subjugated to the pressures of propaganda.

```
LUCKY STRIKE GOES TO WAR--KATE SMITH--BUY WAR BONDS--
GENERAL RANDOLPH SCOTT--MARCH OF TIME--PURPLE HEART--
THIS IS THE ARMY--WILLYS JEEP--HERSHEY BARS--DEAR
JOHN--RITA HAYWORTH
                          THE END
```

World War II films presented and helped preserve widely held values on such basics as war, sex, and drinking. There were no surprises and no dissenting voices. If a character violated the norm, he would be punished. (In reality, of course, people are rarely penalized for wenching, carousing, or drinking too much.)

The communicative strategies were clear-cut and clearly executed. Film-goers were not confused by ambiguous interpretations of ethical points or lack of internal consistency. The central strategy—that men of different origins and backgrounds could be welded together by war—was an all-pervasive one; it was familiar and was generally accepted by audiences without question. (In real war, many men never warmed to their ethnically varied fellows, but palled around only with their own kind.)

In these films, the characterizations were portrayed in clearly delineated and immediately recognizable stereotypes: the Americans were good, the Japs/Germans evil. There were no shades of gray. That the Japanese slaughter women and children must be true because it happened in three previous pictures. In this way, Hollywood created its own war, a war supported by previous battle pictures documenting their interpretation.

Hollywood created myths about men at war that served propaganda purposes, but rarely conformed to reality. The myths of the American sharpshooter or of Japanese torturers were obviously fabrications. The war viewed in theaters by American civilians was not a real one; it was a war which Hollywood scripted and designed.

FILM: POT AND PETER FONDA

There was a certain class of movie-goer who snickered when watching the John Wayne War Epic. While less sophisticated Americans cheered as the fiendish enemy marched into an ambush, the cynic roared with delight at the heavy-handed propaganda. He was well read, bright, and knew when he was being put on. Today, he is in his fifties and admires such films as *Midnight Cowboy, Easy Rider,* and *Husbands.* To this film-goer these productions are monumental, serious indictments of contemporary culture and therefore suitable cocktail conversation.

A Myth Is a Myth

This section will suggest that the former cynic's admiration of contemporary film-making is testimony to the advancement and sophistication of Hollywood's myth-making. While the old Hollywood created legends and fantasies about love and war, the new Hollywood creates the myth that film is the chief producer of the most socioeconomically concerned and unmediated truths about the present generation. Today's films, if examined critically, reveal that the "newness" is to be found in *new stories* rather than in *new artistic conceptions.* In this regard, the film-makers do not produce alternative ways of perceiving the world or art, but simply a presentation of the world as it actually appears. For instance, the factual filming of a revolt at Columbia University may be new in that it is the first time the event is visually chronicled; but this semidocumentary telling of a new story does not necessarily entail an imaginative interpretation or an advancement in film skill and technique.

> No one ever went broke underestimating the taste of the American public.
>
> --H. L. Mencken[4]

Film Truth and History

The strategy of the contemporary film-maker is not directed toward fantasy or illusion, but toward a new cinematic ethic, one which presumably presents the truth about contemporary America. The film director who can best sense the pulse of America and then quickly transform that feeling or fact into a film becomes a success. In addressing this unmasking of America by today's film directors, critic Richard Gilman has observed:

> This morale and manner has meant that the world, hidden for so long behind fantasy and illusion, as though by a conspiracy to keep us from knowing, has come flooding onto the screen, carrying with it every verisimilitudinous gesture and face, all languages and vocabularies of currency, the seemingly authentic violences, pathologies, and pornographies (as well as the stances that have been adopted against them) of the age and event of the moment.[5]

Gilman saw the making of *The Graduate** and *Bonnie and Clyde*† as seemingly the beginning, the starting point when Hollywood decided to look with intensity at the fiber and contradictions of American values and existence. It was at this point in film history when the cameras shifted from sugar-coating and fantasy-making to capture the "historical present."

Benjamin in *The Graduate*, played with disarming confusion by Dustin Hoffman, served as a rallying cry for a Hollywood counterattack on America's decadence. The film seemed to make no attempt to shield the audience from the hypocrisy, false values, and greed of certain segments of

---

The Graduate was directed by Mike Nichols, and is now one of the leading film box-office draws of all time.

†*Bonnie and Clyde*, directed by Arthur Penn, was the glorified account of some Texas bank robbers.

society. The heavy-handed mercantilism of Benjamin's family and friends and
the empty ritualism of the church were the central subjects of portrayal.
Whether Benjamin was being hustled into a corner by the frustrated wife of a
business tycoon or whether the antihero was swinging a religious symbol, a
cross, to ward off his attackers at the church wedding, the film's posture was
anti-Establishment and inclined toward identification with a "new ethic" of
truth.[‡] The box-office receipts also demonstrated to American film-makers
that photographing "history as it is" is better business than making musicals
which cost lots of money and fail.

"First-ness"

What makes this new film strategy work is the director's highly competitive
impulse to be the *first* to present the truth. The audience, in turn, is persuaded that the film is the latest in contemporaneousness and is virtually hot
off the editing table. Not unlike the Walter Winchell-style gossip columnists
who survived on first-ness, the film-makers are racing to be the most relevant
and to break the most taboos. This pursuit can produce some ludicrous film
experiences. *Husbands* was the first American movie to present a vomiting
scene, which lasted a full, tension-ridden twelve minutes. The vomiting was
presented and defended with the air of "We're the first to show this facet of
American life." It was the film *Brewster McCloud*'s fate that it was only the
second to present vomiting. To be sure, the *McCloud* scene was more shocking since it showed the heroine vomiting and then kissing her boyfriend—but
Husbands had already been honest and open about this physiological function.

The struggle to be first is evident in many of the current popular films.
Easy Rider, a motorcycle film which inspired many imitators, purports to
show the truth about the drug culture, bigotry in small Southern towns, and
the enjoyments and hardships of living in communes. Films like *Adam at
6 a.m., Putney Swope,* and *Mash* also contain strong elements of the New
Eventfulness and Reality. The fleeing Adam abandons Los Angeles for what
he imagines will be "realness" in a small town in Middle America where he
finds instead only hypocrisy and mendacity; *Putney Swope* offers a
collection of the latest "in" jokes and stereotyped terminology, while *Mash*
shows through satire the callousness of doctors and nurses in a silly
institution called war. Each of these films is apparently intended to serve as
a window on the world through which audiences can glimpse Truth and hear
the incessant humming of an unfair universe.

[‡]The "new ethic" of truth is a belief in or identification with spontaneity, openness,
naturalness, and romanticism, and a dislike for materialistic concerns. Many of these
characteristics first surfaced in America in the New England transcendentalist movement
during the 1840's; at the turn of the century they were popular among certain anarchists
and socialists.

Film's Manipulative Strategies

What makes the strategy of "filmic truth" especially deceptive is the audience's inability to detect dishonesty in any portion of a particular film. Since the film-maker's heralded intent is to mirror society as it really is today, the normal reaction of the film-viewer is to accept that intent as an honest one and that mirror as a valid reflector. A manipulative factor, however, inevitably obtrudes. The writers and directors of films have to *select* carefully the elements and events to be dramatized, to be emphasized, to be ignored. And by its very nature and intent, such selectivity becomes in itself highly manipulative.

Over-Identification

Events skillfully chosen and ingeniously put together in such a way as to create maximum filmic impact do what they are designed, above all else, to do: *involve* the audience. And the better the film, the greater the involvement. A really good film can involve the viewer so closely that he can come away from the experience with the feeling that he has *actually participated* in the events and circumstances, rather than recognizing that he has experienced them *vicariously.* But, of course, seeing it is *not* the same as doing it; we cannot dismiss the fact of esthetic distance. Put another way, while we may experience subjectively, we can *evaluate* that experience only objectively. The danger of over-identification lies in failure to evaluate film experiences objectively.

A sobering thought is that most of the Reality films express only a limited number of behavioral alternatives. The characters in *Easy Rider* or *Husbands* represent only a slice of society, and are not symbols for all of society. And although the characters are usually believable, they often portray only the radical or reactionary sides of our culture. The moderate or tolerant view frequently is either not depicted or is relegated to a minor role.

Viewers are often confronted with and then manipulated into choosing between only two behavioral alternatives: radical or reactionary. While it is a director's prerogative to narrow the conflict or to focus the issues for dramatic effect, it is the film-goer's option to be stimulated, and yet not be locked into an arbitrary position.

One of the most shocking and powerful film scenes of the early seventies was presented in the film *Joe*, directed by John Avildsen and written by Norman Wexler. After the hardhat Joe and his executive friend Compton are robbed by some hippies, the victims catch the thieves. Joe, who grabs two guns from his car, runs inside the hippie commune and starts shooting. He hands Compton a gun and tells him to choose sides. Compton hesitates—then

chooses Joe's side. Compton shoots several hippies, one of whom—as he and
the audience realize as the movie ends—is his own daughter. For the film-
goer to be forced to choose between the alternatives presented in *Joe*—the
hardhats' position or that of the hippies—seems unfair and unnecessarily
limited. One would like to think that the attitudes of the hardhat, the
executive, and the hippies are not the only ones from which to choose.
Behavioral alternatives to robbing or shooting include calling the police or
forgetting the whole incident.

"You've Seen *It—So* You've Done *It*"

In simplest terms, the manipulation says: "To see it is to have *done* it or to
have *been* it." Many film-goers, especially the young, see for the first time in
films events or experiences which were previously hidden behind closed
doors. When they see the drug culture as depicted in *Easy Rider* they often
believe that they *know* the drug culture. Similarly, in their minds, seeing
social realities as dramatized in *The Graduate* is somehow tantamount to
becoming master and knowledgeable critic of the whole scheme of social
injustice. These *reflected images* of the world as captured on film encourage
in the viewer a frequently erroneous and dangerous feeling that because he
has witnessed the images of screened events, he has directly participated in
the actualities. Nor does the fact that the manipulation is largely self-induced
make it any less dangerous; in fact, it may make it even more potent. This
kind of experience leads the viewer to feel that not only has he participated
in and understood the event, but also to believe that he can now *control* that
event or circumstance. But he cannot. Benjamin, the central catalyst of
The Graduate, is only a mimic of the real world, a device through which the
director-author team projects and reflects a sequence of highly selective
events and manipulative value-judgments. For young Sally Jones of West
Covina to think that because she has sat through *The Graduate* she understands and has even triumphed over hypocrisy is treacherously misleading.
When her father cons her out of marrying the local filling-station attendant
by offering her a Mustang, her subsequent inability to refuse the offer may
well be testimony to the important but inadequately learned lesson of
The Graduate.

Hollywood: The Agent of Truth

A second facet of the strategy of film as truth is the inevitable intertwining
of the film industry and truth-telling. The youthful viewer who grows
accustomed to discovering his reality in film is only one step away from
seeing film as the chief and maybe the only purveyor of truth in our society.

Film becomes the presentational form which alone carries the monumental truths of our time. It is as if we are unable to see history without film.

However, some logical extensions of viewing film as the sole purveyor of truth lead to apparent absurdities:

1. If there were no film, there would be no truth.
2. A film director's perception of the reality of a given event is more accurate than the perception of that event by someone who has actually participated in it.
3. No matter what the event, it does not exist until brought to film.

Why suffer when Benjamin can suffer for you? Why get beaten by cops when *The Strawberry Statement* can show you what it feels like? Why bother to train for an Olympic sport when the hero of *Downhill Racer,* Robert Redford, can take your place? . . . In fact, why bother to get out of the house when all you need is some film and a movie projector?

Things Do Turn Around

The onslaught of so-called reality films and the outpouring of graphic first-ness have produced an inevitable backlash among viewers. Apparently, a film-goer is willing to endure only so much truthfulness before he reverts to fantasy and wish-fulfillment—or *Love Story.* Testimony to this retreat from reality is the overwhelming popularity of Erich Segal's sad retelling of love, found and lost. The mawkish tale of the rich Harvard jock and the poor 'Cliffe co-ed coaxed those same people who loved *The Graduate* into repentant tears.

What made the filming of *Love Story* work was a skillful mixture of the myth and fantasy of the films of the thirties and forties with a gentle leavening of Hollywood reality—but just a leavening. The only semblance of reality was the mention that Oliver was going to work for a civil-rights firm and the faint shadow of the Gulf and Western building as he cast his eyes heavenward in the final scene in the park. For those citizens who find America's urban blight, pollution, race problems, and drug use horrible to ponder, this film was a nice escape. And to enrich the film's lure, the details of *Love Story* were so scanty that escapists could envision themselves lying bravely on the hospital bed or fighting back tears of loss. There were no nasty effects from Jennie's disease; and Oliver was a handsome, tough Harvard jock. The viewer provided his own version of the reality; and this, of course, was far pleasanter to role-play than the societal brutality of *Midnight Cowboy.*

A Final Scenario

The film opens in the Marine Training Center in San Diego. There are the usual troubles getting the new trainees together. The sergeant in charge of raw recruits is played by Jennie's father, who is a poor, but honest Italian from Providence. The "Kid" is played by Oliver Barrett, a star athlete from an uppity eastern school who joined the marines to forget. . . . Somehow we get the feeling that . . . we've been here before.

DESPITE THE PROBLEM OF LEAKS, GRAFFITO IS AN EFFICIENT, FAIRLY SAFE INSTRUMENT OF TRANSMISSION FOR YOUTH. ALMOST ANYTHING ELSE, FROM UNDERGROUND NEWSPAPERS TO MIMEOGRAPHED HANDOUTS, IS MORE LIKELY TO BE READ BY ADULTS.

IN A WORLD OVERBURDENED WITH INFORMATION SOURCES, MOST PEOPLE WOULD NOT SPEND TIME DECIPHERING THE LONELY GRAFFITI. GRAFFITO IS THE COMMUNICATION INSTRUMENT OF THE DISCONTENTED. IT IS FREE, ANONYMOUS, AND WIDELY SPREAD. IT ALSO DEFACES PUBLIC PROPERTY...

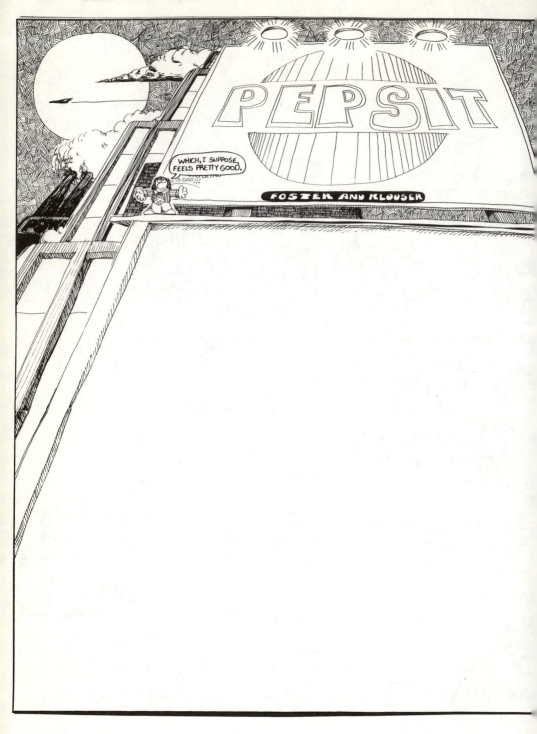

How It Proliferates

"I am not one of those who believe that civilization
has to change in order for the theater to change;
but I do believe that the theater, utilized in the
highest and most difficult sense possible, has the
power to influence the aspect and formation of
things; and the encounter upon the stage of two
passionate manifestations, two living centers, two
nervous magnetisms is something as entire, true,
even decisive as, in life, the encounter of one
epidermis with another in a timeless debauchery."

--Antonin Artaud[1]

"They [Hollywood] reject me, until it makes money at
the box office, then I'm their darling. But they
still hold me in contempt on the one hand and awe
on the other. In contempt, because I've shown them
a mirror of their own greed, and in awe, because I
was able to do something they can't do, which was
simply to make a film honestly."

--Peter Fonda, about Easy Rider[2]

"Should an 8-year old
Worry about cholesterol?"

--Advertisement for Corn Oil Margarine

"My Perfect Martini??
Anchovy Stuffed Olive.
And the Perfect Martini gin,
Gresham's Extra Dry."

"THAT'S IT. A mother-raping white man gets himself
killed up here trying to get his kicks and here we
are, two cops of the inferior race, stuck with
trying to find out who killed him."

--Grave Digger in Hot Day,
Hot Night, by Chester Himes[3]

"Yah, dis heah's de Woofman's album, bay-aay-he-baay! An' you goona love dis rec-uhd ta death, baay-aay-he-aay! An' you send faahv dollahs in cash, check, or monay owh-dah! No c.o.d., bay-buh! An' send it to Uncle Geawge's Recuhd Shop, Chuu-la-Vis-ta, Ca-li-faawn-ya, baay-ay-baay!"

> --Wolfman Jack Show, XERB,
> Tijuana, Mexico, Underground radio

"Today we're beginning to realize that the new media aren't just mechanical gimmicks for creating worlds of illusion, but new language with new and unique powers of expression."

> --Marshall McLuhan[4]

ANGELA
WE LOVE YOU, BABY
> --Bumper sticker

"But how many people were to sit for three hours and forty minutes of bike-riding and dig it? So it came down to the fact that I wanted to communicate. I wanted to reach as many people as possible."

> --Dennis Hopper, on editing the film, Easy Rider[5]

Then came Rudy with his wagonful of tricks.

G is for good and goodness.
E is for evil and evilness.
T is for television and tediousness.
> --Rudy

THE CROTCHLESS PANTY
"He'll really enjoy you in this French-inspired naughty panty with high-cut legs and nothing in the middle but lots of black lace and you! What a delicious way to get his attention!"

> --Department store advertisement

"That rock is a way of life, and verging in this
decade on universal, and can't be stopped, retarded,
put down, muted, modified or successfully controlled
by typeheads, whose arguments don't apply and whose
machinations can't mesh because they don't perceive
(dig) what rock really is and does."

     --Chester Anderson, "Notes for the New Geology"[6]

"Silence is Golden,
but a Noisy Pickle
is a Crisp Pickle."
                    --Pickle commercial

"This should be a theatre of World Spirit. Where
the spirit can be shown to be the most competent
force in the world. Force. Spirit. Feeling. The
language will be anybody's, but tightened by the
poet's backbone. And even the language must show
what the facts are in this consciousness epic, what's
happening. We will talk about the world, and the
preciseness with which we are able to summon the
world will be our art. Art is method. And art,
'like any ashtray or senator,' remains in the world.
Wittgenstein said ethics and aesthetics are one. I
believe this."

--LeRoi Jones[7]

Preface
Number Three

I wrote this book for the money and the academic promotions it will afford. That I have anything to say is incidental—I wrote the book out of self-interest. I wrote, typed, and edited it myself. Any errors are the fault of my publisher, whose lack of good taste is astounding. To my colleagues, Professors Brooks, Griffin, Haiman, and Wood, a reminder that I will be dropping into the office twice a week. To my students, who mostly cut my lectures, and who—when they attended—heckled, hissed, and booed, a reminder that I am making 29 cents a copy for the stuff they thought trash. To my wife and children, who nagged, pestered, and complained while I wrote this book, a reminder that the book is not dedicated to them. And to those would-be authors who will attempt to plagiarize my material—I have placed a curse on you.

Irving J. Rein
Northwestern University

HOW THEY MAKE IT
SECTION THREE

IN THE FILM <u>THE GRADUATE</u>, A GUEST'S ADVICE TO YOUNG BENJAMIN ON HOW TO MAKE IT WAS "PLASTICS." AT ONE TIME OR ANOTHER, THE ADVICE FOR NEW GRADUATES HAS BEEN "RAILROADS," "OUTBOARD MOTORS," "REAL ESTATE," OR "MUNICIPAL BONDS." IT IS ALSO LEGENDARY FOR ADULTS (ESPECIALLY THOSE WHO HAVE NOT MADE IT) TO SUGGEST MARRYING FOR MONEY.

IF I WERE YOU I'D MARRY THAT ELDRED GIRL. AFTER FIVE YEARS THEY ALL LOOK THE SAME ANYWAY.

SAY, COULD I INTEREST YOU IN SOME MUNICIPAL BONDS?

FOR SALE

SOME VOCATIONS FOR MAKING IT, SUCH AS EVANGELISM, ARE STRICTLY CYCLICAL. PERIODS SUCH AS THE 1920'S ARE EXCELLENT TIMES TO DON A WHITE ROBE, RENT A WHITE CADILLAC, AND TOUR THE SOUTH IN A REVIVAL TENT MEETING. THIS SECTION CONCERNS CITIZENS WHO HAVE MADE IT AND ALSO TELLS **HOW** TO MAKE IT.

YOU WILL LEARN IN THIS SECTION HOW SOME INDIVIDUALS HAVE, THROUGH SOME OF THE COMMUNICATION SKILLS DISCUSSED, TRAVELED THE SOMETIMES DEVIOUS ROUTE FROM "WE" TO "THEY." WHEN "THEY" GO BACK TO REUNIONS, PEOPLE WILL RECOGNIZE IMMEDIATELY THAT "THEY" MADE IT IN _____

FOR INSTANCE, SOME PEOPLE WHO HAVE MADE IT: JOE NAMATH, MILO MINDERBINDER, FRANK ZAPPA, RICHARD BURTON, BOB DYLAN, RUSS MEYER, JESSE JACKSON, PAT NIXON, ED McMAHON, NORMAN MAILER, MINNESOTA FATS, MYRON COHEN, BETTY FRIEDAN, BURT BACHARACH, COLONEL SANDERS, RONALD REAGAN, BILLY GRAHAM, ARNOLD PALMER, RALPH NADER, GLORIA STEINEM, AND ELLIOT GOULD.

YOUR NAME GOES HERE

I'VE MADE IT

SOME NOTABLE EXAMPLES OF NOT MAKING IT: SOUPY SALES, STANLEY KOWALSKI, JAMES LING, NORMAN PODHORETZ, GARY CROSBY, HUBERT HUMPHREY, WILLIAM WESTMORELAND, KANDY KANE, ZSA ZSA GABOR, LINDSAY NELSON, MARK RUDD, PHIL EVERLY, DAGMAR, JERRY LEWIS, PORTNOY, MARY TYLER MOORE, AND H. RAP BROWN.

YOUR NAME SCRAWLED HERE!!

BUT OF COURSE WE CAN'T ALL MAKE IT.

12 The Rhetoric of the Car Lot

In the ancient art of rhetoric, few orators will be forever emulated and revered. The power of Pericles, the flattery of Cicero, the strength of Robespierre, the style of Lincoln—in each the quintessence of a rhetorical skill is captured often for only a moment but, nonetheless, captured. Where are the great masters of oratory today? I have studied Isocrates, Aristotle, Longinus, and Cicero, seeking in all of them the cardinal principles of rhetoric which would provide a clue to the identity of today's masters.

I had almost abandoned my search. Then, one day while I rummaged amidst ancient canons in the library, a wizened old man suddenly appeared in the stacks. "Go to Fritzie's Chevrolet," he muttered.

"No, thank you," I answered. "I'm happy with my Olds . . ."

"Go see Barney Jullip. He has studied with the masters." Then, with a condescending nod, he clarified: "He is the Babe Ruth of Rhetoric."

The Master

Mr. Jullip and I discussed salesmanship as we walked through the new car showroom at Fritzie's. When we reached a hugger orange Camaro with four-speed and rally wheels, he turned to me and asked, "Where will the new men come from? Salesmanship is dead in this country." Profound and terse commentary—typical characteristics, I later discovered, of Jullip's eloquence.

"I learned everything from the Golden Greek," recalled Barney.

"Aristotle or Plato?" I queried.

"I mean the greatest car salesman in the history of Chicago, George Karatopolos." And Barney told me of the man who brought automobile selling to its greatest heights in the twenties, when Karatopolos allegedly sold mobster Al Capone six bullet-proof Lincolns at list price. Barney maintains that Karatopolos' arrival in America in 1910 was to the automobile industry what physicist Albert Einstein's arrival from Germany was to the Atomic Age. "He brought eloquence to this country and made automobile selling what it is today."

Barney uses a straightforward strategy in selling automobiles. "I bust their goddam heads open." Unlike Abraham Lincoln, Jullip sometimes resorts to expletive instead of precision. "I go two ways, to the pocket and to the head. I destroy the sonofabitch. Everyone treats the customer like he's a fragile piece of merchandise. . . . 'How are you? . . . Nice day. . . . May I help you? . . . Can I show you our latest models?' That's what the customer wants to hear. I wouldn't give him the satisfaction. He's the snake and I'm the mongoose. I swallow the sonofabitch."

At this point, he was interrupted by a customer. (Later, I learned his name was Samuel Berger.)

"Hi," said Barney, rather hostilely.

"Hello," responded a middle-aged man with a defiant air.

"What are you looking for?"

"A car."

"Big or small?"

"A . . . a small car."

"Got a trade?"

"A '66 Impala."

"How much do you want for it? Sit down!"

"Thank you. Ah . . . $1300."

"You got a deal!"

"Huh? I was just—"

"I got a small car for you, and I will give you $1300. How much money you got?"

"$90-$100, but—"

"Good, give it to me." (Reaches for customer's pocket.)

"Ah . . ." (Protecting his pocket.) "I was just shopping. . . . I've got to talk to my wife."

"Listen!" (Jabs finger at customer's chest.) "This is my livelihood. This isn't some kind of game. I wouldn't insult you at your business. I'll find a nice, small car with automatic transmission, power steering—blue, green, anything you want. Here, I'll give you a receipt. How about a coke?"

This dialogue is the famous Jullip opening barrage. Not unlike Winston Churchill's memorable "Blood, Sweat, and Tears" speech, the strategy is based on the assumption that people want to be led and dominated. In moments of crisis, many war-torn citizens and shoppers want the control of a strong leader. Jullip fills the vacuum of leadership by assaulting and bewildering the Sunday shopper and ending his worries by putting him into a new car. Samuel Berger happened to be the exception. He walked out. Jullip shrugged, unshaken.

"The jerk wants to be sold," claims Jullip. "It's a battle for the mind, and I will win. They're a bunch of animals—and so am I."

Another notorious Jullip strategy is the "I'm crazy—I quit—you lose" tactic. "What do you mean, I'm too high? I'm giving you the sled [car] at fifty bucks over cost, and you're trying to chisel me. I quit. I've had it. Twenty years in this business and some fag cracks me!" With that line, Jullip rises from his desk, seizes a ball point pen, and hurls it against the plate glass window. Then he frantically gallops around the showroom, yanking and spilling desk drawers while bellowing, "Twenty years in the business, and I finally go *meshuga*!" Abruptly, he then self-righteously strides to his desk, empties it, and exits.

After Jullip's departure, the bewildered customer is approached by Leon G., an elderly gray-haired salesman whose last name no one can pronounce. With a gentle European accent, he addresses the stunned customer. "Pardon me, sir. I am a personal friend of Mr. Jullip. Let me explain his unusual behavior." Leon seats the victim and recites the long history of Mr. Jullip's heart attacks and subsequent mental depressions. In less than ten minutes, the now contrite customer purchases an accessory laden barge at a healthy profit to the seller. The customer just "lays down"[*] and will

---

[*]A *lay down* is a customer who offers no resistance and is eager to buy.

pay anything, as an act of penance. While Leon completes the sale, Mr. Jullip enjoys coffee in the backroom and wonders how much of a take he will split with Leon G.

Although Jullip executes this strategy well, it is not unique. Other rhetoricians also have used the strategy with success. Adolf Hitler ranted and raved for years—and each time, the confused Western nations capitulated to the apparent raving maniac.

Adolf Hitler is alive and well and selling Volkswagens in Argentina.

The Identifier

The most accomplished one-shot strategist at Fritzie's is Bob Ranaway, the identifier. Unlike Jullip, he does not have a variety of persuasive gems to apply to different situations. Instead, he has one strategy—he identifies. "What you are, I am," says Bob.

"Hi, I'm Bob Ranaway."
"Hello, I'm Emil Haapasaari."
"No kidding!"
"Huh?"
"My wife is Finnish, too. Comes from a small town of Finns in northern Minnesota."
"Well, I'll be darned! Say, do you know Harold Paavola?"
"I'm sure my wife does. . . ."

"Hi, I'm Bob Ranaway. Hot, isn't it?"
"Not for us! We're from Alabama."
"No kidding? . . . Well, it's sure a pleasure up here in the unfriendly North to meet . . ."

"Let's go out to the back lot, and I'll show you some convertibles."
"I'd rather sit here because of my ticker. I had a cardiac arrest back in the spring of '64 and been taking it easy ever since."
"Yeah? I've been on digitalis for six months! Who's your doctor?"

The intent of Ranaway's strategy is to take the encounter out of the sales category and put it into the realm of good friends having a pleasurable conversation. Ranaway makes no hard sales pitch; in fact, he talks little money or service. His strategy is to spend half an hour reminiscing about aching backs, flooding basements, or vacationing in the Ozarks, followed by two or three minutes to wrap up the sale.

Ranaway is one in a long line of distinguished orators who have used this strategy. For years, midwestern politicians have identified with farmers by recalling childhood days spent in shucking corn and pitching hay. But nowhere in the history of public address is there mention of a speaker with Ranaway's skill of identifying. Neither Henry Clay nor William Jennings Bryan could find so many areas with which to identify.

In an unguarded moment, Ranaway said of his skill: "In a way, I am all of these people. That's what makes me effective, and others mere imitators."

The Professional

I hailed Samuel Berger as he walked from the Fritzie showroom. "Why did you leave in the midst of the Jullip oratory?"

He smiled. "I'm from the L.A. school—I prefer subtlety. Let me take you to the greatest speaker of them all."

Soon we were face to face with Harold Smith, one of Chrysler's finest. Berger whispered, "Observe the wit, the chivalry, the careful and gradual shift to money." I was skeptical, but I watched carefully.

"Mr. Berger! How are you, sir? Please sit down! A new Chrysler? I would be pleased to show you our new selections." Berger smiled as Harold trotted out facts and figures, chassis charts, color selections—all with remarkable aplomb. He certainly was a professional, with none of Jullip's chicanery. But could he sell cars?

The price was $3600. Berger countered with $2650. Smith, with a raised eyebrow, suggested $3300. The battle was stalemated at $3135.

Smith said, "Sign."

Berger said, "Give me twenty-four hours."

Smith, his cool seemingly ready to evaporate, accused Berger of not trusting him, to which Berger cruelly agreed. That prompted Smith to lament: "And how about customers who try to buy cars at below cost and force the salesman to be dishonest to make a living?" The hook was sunk. Berger slumped in his chair.

"Where do I sign," he whimpered.

I wanted to throw flowers. What a brilliant performance! When I queried Smith about it, he smiled modestly. "I'm a professional like a doctor or a lawyer. People like my self-confidence, subtlety, and good taste."

"Then you never lie?"

"When it comes to money, I never tell the truth."

"Do you mean during this sophisticated approach you fudge on price?"

"Listen, everyone wants something for nothing. My elegant performance reinforces the credibility of my price statement—but I never tell the truth."

"Do you know of Jullip?"

"He's too crude. Blows too many people out the door."

The phone rang. "How much is a four-door Newport hardtop with automatic transmission, power steering, power brakes, tinted glass, and special wheel covers?"

"Oh, that will run you about $1850."

"Gee, everyone else wants at least $2900. Why are you so cheap?"

"Because we do a big volume."

"I'll be right down."

Five minutes later the phone shopper appears.

"Is Mr. Smith here? Hi! I called about the Newport for $1850."

"I just sold it." (The customer's face falls in stunned disbelief.) "But fortunately I have another car which is much nicer for a little more money."

"At this point," said Smith, in an aside to me, "the skill of the salesman is important. The customer would not have come down if he had received an accurate price over the phone. He knows he can't buy that car for $1850, but he has to be manipulated into paying more. So you twist and turn him until he eagerly hands over $2900 for a similar car."

"How do you get a customer up from $1850 to $2900?"

"Oh, in a variety of ways. Hit him with freight and transportation— that's worth a couple of hundred."

"But isn't that already figured in the $2900?"

"Of course. But many people never notice. Another device is to switch cars. Get him into a New Yorker for a higher price, since we're 'temporarily' out of Newports. If he objects, point out that the Newport has an inadequate body frame and is dangerous. I usually tell him that because of his family he would be a murderer to buy the car. It's called switching, and it usually works."

Smith, not unlike Woodrow Wilson, presents a highly professional image to his audiences. If Wilson had only had Smith's diction!

The Butcher

Timothy Gordon is an out-and-out thief who specializes in used cars. Unlike Jullip, Ranaway, or Smith, he has no guile. For the intelligent customer, Gordon is little worry because he operates on such a base level.

"This Corvette will cost you $6000 plus $2000 federal road tax."

"Hey, I've been buying cars for years and haven't ever paid a road tax."

"Have you ever bought a 'Vette before?"

"No."

"Well, you pay a road tax."

Or, the Gordon-Missing-Parts Ruse:

"I want an air-conditioned '66 for $900."

"I've got one, but don't tell the boss that I sold it so cheap."

So, Mr. Bargain Hunter drives out in his '66 Buick Riviera with factory air, thinking, "I finally screwed a salesman." When the temperature hits 90 degrees, he expectantly turns on the cool blast, but gets an empty click. The car has vents, but no air.

"The jerk won't come back," says Gordon. "He doesn't want to appear more stupid than everyone knows he is already."

Gordon talked also of the freight-and-transportation gimmick, and of customer embarrassment. "The average guy goes shopping without his wife, and then brings her along later, when he thinks he's found a good deal. If you say the car is $2300 and he remembers $2100, he is going to look like a fool before his wife if he argues. And, of course, when you tack on $150 for F-and-T, he doesn't want to appear ignorant by asking what it is for and if it is legal."

Though he lacks Jullip's showmanship, Ranaway's common-ground . conviviality, and Smith's smoothness, Gordon probably is the most economical of all the master orators. He finds his adversaries' weaknesses; then, swiftly and without ceremony, he executes the appropriate strategy. That he is larcenous only reaffirms the fact that he models himself after a long line of political orators.

Notes on Selling

Three Kinds of Customers

1. The "laydown"—comes prancing into the showroom, title card in pocket, and buys eagerly. Be nice to him, since there are only a few left.

2. The "shopper"—out for a Sunday visit. Grab him off the merry-go-round and sell him a car.

3. The "haggler"—enjoys the combat. He is nice to his family, but goes wild when near a showroom. Claw him, chew him, and put him in a car.

Four Pricing Strategies

1. Start high and let the customer knock you down. He likes to hear the thud of prices hitting a succession of imagined "bottoms."

2. Start low, get his money, and then work the price up with F-and-T, undercoating, and car switching.

3. Get him off the previous dealer's price by switching the car or the equipment.

4. Give him a fair price. Probably it won't get you a sale, but it will give your colleagues a few laughs.

5. *Reminder!* Always control the customer by limiting the number of alternatives he can choose among:

    A.   Buy today. There's a special price if you do. Many customers have bought cars when convinced by salesmen that the price would be higher tomorrow.

    B.   Qualify the customer by asking a series of questions: own a car? got any money? got a trade-in?

    C.   You've got the car. Make the customer work to get it from *you*.

    D.   Establish control over the customer by leading him around the showroom. A customer, if asked and then firmly directed by the salesman, will go anywhere and do anything. When you are explaining to the customer about the ceramic-coated muffler, urge him to crawl under the car to see the muffler glow. When the customer questions durability, instruct him to climb into the trunk and jump up and down. He will do everything you ask him to. Finally, you will ask him to sign; and his signing will be the natural culmination of your control.

Notes on Defending Yourself

Greed is the downfall of most car buyers. Generally, if a customer concedes that a dealer is entitled to a $150 profit, he isn't as susceptible to being "taken" as is the buyer who is looking for a car for nothing. Telephone calling for low prices is a waste of time, as is going to twenty different dealers.

The best strategy is to find the exact car and equipment you want, check *Edmund's* New or Used Car guide[†] for exact cost, select from three to five dealers, and work them for the lowest price. Specifically:

1. Never be switched from a car and equipment you have selected. Do

---

[†]There are a number of car price books which are sold on newsstands and which will give the prospective buyer a good idea what his new or used car should cost.

not abandon a vinyl roof if that is what you want. If a salesman does not have exact equipment, get up and leave.

2. Tell the salesman you are a buyer and want a low price.

3. If the salesman starts using some of the strategies mentioned in this book, tell him you know what he is doing: "Stop identifying and get on with the price." Or simply enjoy the pitch and *then* tell him.

4. Don't believe anything the salesman says. He doesn't believe anything *you* say.

5. Never buy a car without first seeing it.

49   PONTIAC

Year's Model Body Type	Original List Price	Current Average Wholesale	Current Average Retail	Year's Model Body Type	Original List Price	Current Average Wholesale	Current Average Retail
1969				**1968**			
FIREBIRD 6*				**TEMPEST 6***			
Hardtop Coupe	2814	2025	2450	2 Door Sport Sedan	2438	1300	1675
Convertible	3028	2075	2500	4 Door Sedan	2485	1325	1700
TEMPEST 6*				**TEMPEST CUSTOM 6***			
Sports Coupe	2493	1725	2125	2 Door Hardtop	2591	1575	1950
4 Door Sedan	2540	1750	2150	2 Door Coupe	2531	1425	1800
				4 Door Hardtop	2810	1550	1925
CUSTOM 'S' 6*				4 Door Sedan	2579	1475	1850
Sports Coupe	2586	1850	2275	Convertible	2839	1525	1900
4 Door Sedan	2634	1900	2325	2 Seat Wagon	2883	1700	2100
Hardtop Coupe	2648	2000	2425				
4 Door Hardtop	2760	2025	2450	**LE MANS 6***			
Convertible	2871	2075	2500	2 Door Hardtop	2763	1700	2100
2 Seat Wagon	2939	2150	2600	Sport Coupe	2701	1525	1900
				4 Door Hardtop	2893	1725	2125
LE MANS 6*				Convertible	3015	1700	2100
Sports Coupe	2756	1975	2400				
Hardtop Coupe	2818	2150	2600	**SAFARI 6***			
4 Door Hardtop	2948	2200	2650	2 Seat Wagon	3084	1775	2175
Convertible	3047	2225	2675				
Safari	3181	2275	2775	**FIREBIRD 6***			
				Hardtop	2758	1825	2250
*For 8 cylinder models add $100 wholesale. and retail.				Convertible	2996	1850	2275

*For 8 cylinder models add $100 wholesale. and retail.

The Amateur

After my intensive investigation of automobile salesmanship, I decided to sell cars myself. If this is where the great oratory is being practiced, I should be involved. I told the general manager of Fritzie's that I was a professional closer from Boston.

"May I help you? . . . Listen, the car costs $3150, but I'll sell it to you for $2925. . . . Why not? I don't need the money. I make my living being a college professor."

HOW MANY?

Show about three items.

The customer will let you know her prefer-ence. She may buy *more than one* and in-crease your sale.

WHAT PRICE?

Concentrate on middle and top priced mer-chandise. Increase your sales by "TRAD-ING-UP." Encourage her to charge it.

SUBSTITUTES?

If you don't have what she wants, show her a similar item that you think will suit her needs.

Selling Tips Help your customer make an intelligent choice.

13 How to Make It in Dissent

Many of life's endeavors lend themselves to "making it." A young person can make it in fried chicken franchises, selling custom stereo consoles, manufacturing plastic toy pistols, "busting" blocks of real estate near ghettos, and in a number of other traditional avenues to success. In these fields, by working hard, occasionally cheating a little, and not being caught in an immoral act with one of your data processors or salesclerks, you can quite possibly be a success.

This "making it" may mean an opulent apartment, a fashionable wardrobe, Sunday brunches, ski trips to Aspen, and a red Ferrari. This kind of success is recognized by most Americans as either crass or laudable—but it is nonetheless recognized.

This chapter considers the strategies of making it in certain areas of endeavor not traditionally recognized as avenues of ascent. Specifically, we will examine how three individuals in public life have successfully capitalized upon dissent either by (1) flamboyant and well-timed association with it, or by (2) promoting and exploiting it for personal profit, or by (3) politically defending the Establishment against it.

These three public figures were quick to recognize dissent as a *marketable commodity.* The media, as we have noted several times before in this book, cover riots and protests more eagerly than they cover church picnics or Eagle Scout Award nights. Clearly, any public activity that vigorously assails widely held patterns of conduct is going to receive a healthy share of media attention. As a consequence, dissent has become big business. Opportunistic individuals study anti-Establishment sentiments, determine which ones are the newest and most viable, and proceed to devise services and products of potential use to the fledgling anarchist or the curious citizen. Daniel Cohn-Bendit, the red-haired radical who led the revolt of French students in the late sixties couldn't resist writing a best-seller about his experiences.[1] The revenue from his chronicle of revolution financed a life style which made him the envy of other European radicals. Hollywood, with its talent for grabbing onto popular trends, very quickly began to produce revolution films saturated with sit-ins, bombings, and police brutality. *Zabriskie Point, The Strawberry Statement,* and *Getting Straight* character-ized the genre. Clothing manufacturers who made their last killing with the Batman craze began to turn out T-shirts emblazoned with "OFF THE PIG." When Post or Kellogg finally introduces Dissent Cereal, which has to be flogged, spat upon, and gassed before becoming edible, the Revolution probably will be over.

This chapter poses a three-part analysis of the communication skills of three men who have made it in dissent:

Litterateur Norman Mailer
Yippie Leader Abbie Hoffman
Chicago's Mayor Richard Daley

When Mailer, Hoffman, and Daley attend their high-school reunions, they are surrounded by admiring classmates who whisper to their partners: "He really made it!"

Norman Mailer

Mailer began to speak, his pace quickening into a tommy-gun cadence:

```
"Toback, there's a revolution coming, and we're
gonna need you.  I'm gonna need you.  You've got
```

to get all the shit out of your system. You've
gotta find everything good in you and cultivate it.
You have to be your best. Every minute. I'm the
leader of this revolution, see, but I may not be
around long; say in five years I'll be gone. They
may even get me before then. And you have to be
ready to take over."

"Right," I said. "I will."

I was so happy to hear him extravagant again that
I had dropped my hands and left myself open for a
terrific uppercut.

"But the revolution's going to suffer when you
take over, see, because there's a difference
between you and me, Toback, and the difference is
that you're a schmuck and I'm not."

Eight . . . Nine . . . Ten. Out.

Dwight Macdonald walked over, put his arm
around Mailer and they began to talk. I waited a
few seconds and then left.

                    --James Toback, Esquire[2]

Little in communication theory is not exhibited in the art of publicity—
that is, how to achieve (preferably free of charge) "ink," "space," "coverage,"
or anything else that is self-aggrandizing. Norman Mailer is an expert in this
art, conducted in the spirit of protest, but in the name of Norman. See
Norman fighting with Jose Torres, then light-heavyweight champion of the
world—four pages of color pictures in *Life*. See Norman standing on the
steps of the Pentagon—four pages of color pictures in *Look*. See Norman
running for mayor of New York City—*Life, Look*, the *New York Times*, the
Des Moines Register.

Norman Mailer, after his early success as a novelist, is now a social critic
who takes on the Establishment. He has successfully redefined himself as a
novelist who now chronicles major contemporary events in a literary style.
Armed with his "finely tuned sensibilities" and mordant metaphors, he
attacks society's hangups: taboos against dirty words, Puritan sexual
standards, creeping materialism, and White Anglo-Saxon Protestantism.
What distinguishes Mailer from the ordinary social critic is his ability to
convince media to give his remarks more attention than they give those of
the other critics. He gains this coverage by being a special person who is
likely to say or do anything:

Norman says in his Bar Mitzvah speech that he would
like to follow in the footsteps of "great Jews like
Moses Maimonides and Karl Marx."[3]

Norman says, again and again, that orgasm is "the
inescapable existential moment."[4]

Norman stabs his wife "and [gets] away with it,"[5]
goes to Bellevue for observation, flies gliders,
makes movies, runs for President, takes drugs. Yet
Norman's mother has five book shelves of her son's
work.[6]

There are people in public life who like to box, skin dive, wrestle, and
engage in similar exertions which indicate masculinity. When Mailer boxed
Torres, he made some special preparations. He had his press agent call a
number of magazines to ask them if they would like pictures of litterateur
Mailer being swatted about by the best fighter, pound for pound, in
captivity. So there was beetle-browed, paunchy Mailer sticking left jabs,
ducking right hooks, and generally exhibiting the pugilistic skill of a fading
welterweight. Up went sales of Norman's books and down went the
competitors' sales. The book dollar goes only so far.

Possibilities for extending Mailer's publicity techniques seem endless.
Why doesn't Kurt Vonnegut fight Joe Frazier, or John Barth wrestle Haystack
Calhoun? A stunning judo match between Arthur Hailey and James Michener
would settle who is the more thorough researcher. The weakness with
Vonnegut, Barth, Hailey, and Michener is that they lack Mailer's brilliant,
strategical mind for inventing intriguing, newsworthy events. What does
Barth look like?

Norman Mailer knows, for example, that the national magazines devour
material at a ferocious rate, and that they always are looking for fresh copy.
Mailer's strategy is to be colorful and profane, but not too eager with the
media. People who cover news are leery of the eager, too aggressive writer
who wants to promote his next book. Norman handles this wariness by
handling reporters roughly and with little compassion:

"Whose questions are those? They aren't real
questions, they are dull, stupid questions. Why
do you need an interview, you've been here two
weeks. Why are you so greedy? You reporters all
have tapeworm, and the tapeworm is dialogue."[7]

He also delivers his opinions in staccato, seemingly straightforward, quotable
sentences which make good lead stories: "Very few people understand the
Jews, but I do, because I'm one of them." "Governor Maddox has the face
of a three-month-old infant who is mean and bald and wears eyeglasses."
Instead of being angry at Mailer's rudeness and rough language, the press
admires and respects him for his honesty.

Norman Mailer is a man not lacking in talent. He has written five novels, made at last count three full-length movies, and won the Pulitzer Prize for *Armies of the Night*, an account of the 1967 march on the Pentagon. He seems to be wherever the action is—in Washington, Miami, Chicago, New York—marching, sitting-in, rallying, and brawling. When the protest is over, Mailer sits down and chronicles the event in a readable, irreverent style. When the protest is over, moreover, it is hard to remember anyone but Mailer, the chronicler and metaphor-maker. Norman makes a lot of money.

Abbie Hoffman

> I write longhand in the tradition of Hemingway and Mailer, whom I admire.
> —Abbie Hoffman[8]

Abbie Hoffman, leader of the Yippies, is, like Norman Mailer, a master of the outrageous and a leader in the battle against the Establishment. And, to complete the parallel, both Norman and Abbie are authors. It surprised a few revolutionary purists to discover that Abbie, who was active in the march on the Pentagon, the Columbia University strike, and helped create the Battle of Chicago, has cashed in on dissent with two best sellers: *Revolution for the Hell of It* and *Woodstock Nation*. Hoffman's books, the former written under the pseudonym "Free," are mind-blowing contradictions. The books are anything but free; the price for *Woodstock Nation* is $5.95 clothbound and $2.95 paperbound. If you want to quote from Abbie's book, the price is heavy despite his encouragement to use anything you would like to use. Anyone who considers taking Abbie up on his offer—that is, not requesting permission to use his material—is warned not to; in the front of his book is the usual copyright notice:

All rights reserved. No part of this book may be reproduced in any form without the prior written permission of the publisher.

Hoffman beseeches his readers to give up materialism, to steal, fornicate, and be happy, while he "sits-in" in a small Random House office and grinds out copy for thousands of dollars. I can envision Hoffman opening his own publishing company called "Screw You," and hiring Ronald Reagan and Barry Goldwater as coeditors. After all, just because you are involved in a revolution doesn't mean you can't make a little bread!

Following are what seem to be Hoffman's four strategies for making it in dissent, with accompanying rationale:

1. *Be where dissent is brewing.* Even if you have nothing to do with the protest, be there, crazed with anger. When the media people arrive, act as if you are planning strategy, which can change from day to day. This posture assures a return visit by media the following day.

> *Example:* Hoffman generally jets to disturbances with the same aplomb
> as the President or Jacqueline Kennedy Onassis jet around the world.
> He deplanes to scores of press and television reporters, who are waiting
> for his analysis of the crisis. When he finally settles down to be inter-
> viewed, he launches into a wild, maniacal tirade promising to pollute the
> city's water supply with LSD or to hold mass orgies on its fair beaches.
> Whether the newsmen are convinced or think it is a put-on, they give
> the interview lots of space because the public loves it.

2. *Always wear funny costumes.* The Establishment likes this kind of entertainment, and the clothes will create attention. The Yippie official uniform is battered jeans, old moccasins or boots, long hair, rope belts, and an occasional flowered hat.

> *Example:* When Hoffman was summoned before the House Committee
> on Un-American Activities (HUAC), he arrived as an Indian with
> feathers, hunting knife, and a bullwhip. He amused the congressmen
> by playing with an electric Yo-Yo during the questioning.

3. *Swear—Swear—Swear!* Norman and Abbie use lots of swearwords in their books. Americans have a certain fondness for people who say or write naughty words. But neither Norman nor Abbie is ever offensive—just cute. By swearing, you expose the hypocrisy of the whole language system and get porno-lovers to buy the book. In *Revolution for the Hell of It*, Abbie offers an example of this strategy:

```
I think he is a right-wing heckler, and we're
having a fist fight when the blue boys arrive.  It
seems he is a plain-clothesman.  Before I know it
I'm standing in the 16th Precinct, and Badge
#26466, who has missed some of the action, kicks me
in the nuts. . . .
     All the cops are aching for blood.  One is yelling
how his brother got killed in Vietnam and challenges
anybody to a fight in the back alley.  They call us
"scum-bags" and "fairies" and "Jew-bastards" and
"commies" and one says, "You pull dese guys' pants
off and they ain't got no pecker, just a little
piece of flesh."  There are other swears that I
couldn't even recognize because of the culture gap
but it seems they sure got this sex hang-up.  Pretty
soon we're all herded into a van.9
```

4. Stage extravagant demonstrations which are rooted in the Hollywood tradition.   Acquire a reputation for knowing how to put together lively, exciting protests that are both efficient and colorful.

Example: Hoffman and his co-leader Jerry Rubin (who cashed in with *Do It!*) spend a great amount of time seeing that each aspect of their demonstrations has the proper *glitz* or showmanship. A particularly rewarding staging was a frantic dance in front of the New York Stock Exchange to celebrate the end of money. The culmination was the burning of a five-dollar bill. There is some suspicion that Hoffman in an earlier era might have gone into silent movies. He denies rumors that he saves his press clippings.

Abbie Hoffman has a B.A. from Brandeis and an M.A. in psychology from Berkeley. He has been divorced and has remarried. As Abbie himself tells it, he has been a movie-theater manager, a grinder in an airplane factory, a camp counselor, and a drug salesman, among other things. His father, speaking on national television, said that he could not understand the strange ways of his son, but that was before Abbie published his books. Abbie writes fairly well, is a good showman, and has good timing for news events. Obviously, Abbie made an intelligent career choice in selecting revolution as a profession. He is suited for little else and will probably make a nice living.

Richard J. Daley

> Gentlemen, get the thing straight. The policeman isn't there to create disorder; the policeman is there to preserve disorder [sic]. When I ask you as a law-abiding citizen not to proceed any further and you link arms . . . and someone in your outfit kicks him in the groin or spits at him . . . or hits him with a bag of urine or a bag of a four-letter word that begins with S and ends with T, what would *you* do? I just wonder what you'd do.
>
> —Mayor Daley's first press conference after "The Battle of Chicago"[10]

By most standards of success, Mayor Richard Daley of Chicago was in 1968 a giant among urban mayors. Only two years after he became mayor in 1955, *Fortune* Magazine selected him as one of the nine outstanding mayors

Peace movement 'betrayed' by radicals, says McGovern

WASHINGTON (UPI) — Sen. George McGovern (D-S.D.), an outspoken opponent of the Vietnam war, says the peace movement has been betrayed by young radicals who plant bombs, provoke courtroom disorders and wave Viet Cong flags.

"This kind of reckless political action may be enjoyable for affluent youth cut off from the real world, but it is a grave injustice to those who seek an end to war and misery," McGovern said in a letter to several hundred young people who served as summer interns in the House and Senate.

McGovern, coauthor of an amendment designed to end a U.S. combat role in the war by

Dec. 31, 1971, said the "tactics and wild rhetoric" of young revolutionaries such as Yippies Jerry Rubin and Abbie Hoffman have undercut their own cause.

McGOVERN singled out radical leader Tom Hayden as unreasoning and dishonest in his statements about the release from jail of Black Panther Huey Newton.

"In claiming that Panther leader Huey Newton was released from prison because of the guerrilla kidnapers of Uruguay and Brazil, Hayden has gone beyond the limits of either reason or honesty," McGovern said.

And in glorifying the kidnaping and fatal shooting of a California judge by black radi-

cals, McGovern said Hayden "endorses the very barbarism that he professes to dispise."

Hayden made the statements at a recent congress of the National Student Assn. in St. Paul.

McGovern said Newton was freed because "an American court gave him the beneficial protection of our judicial system and found error in his trial."

McGOVERN told the interns that Rubin and Hoffman "by doing their own thing" have become personalities who can command lucrative fees — at the expense of discrediting the peace movement.

"The great weakness of many American radicals . . . is

that their vision is limited only to the weakness of our society. Even though their own freedom depends on the American legal and political system, they use that freedom to proclaim the worthlessness of the system that makes their protest possible."

in the United States. In 1966, he was elected by a vote of 73 percent of the electorate and won all fifty wards in the city. Yet, despite his local power and national prominence, Daley had not consistently received heavy television and magazine coverage. It took the 1968 National Democratic Convention and the mayor's seeming manipulation of events for him to make it.

The extent of Daley's making it can be determined by comparing the total number of national magazine stories about him in 1967 (3) to those in 1968 (33), when he got his lucky break.[11] In all fairness, his story count was helped in the spring of 1968 by his directive to police to "shoot to kill" arsonists and "shoot to maim" looters during rioting in the city. But the mayor's coup occurred when he convinced the Democratic National Committee to hold its convention in Chicago despite the bus/taxi/telephone strikes, and the impending invasion of thousands of dissenters. It was an opportunity for Daley to show America what a big-league mayor could do about law and order.

The scenario at the 1968 convention is well known: thousands of demonstrators and police battling in the Chicago streets amidst MACE, tear gas, swinging clubs, and barbed wire. Television coverage of the monotonous convention inside was frequently broken by switching cameras to mob scenes and shotgun blasts. It was a wild scene for the millions watching in their living rooms, and public reaction was swift. Previously scheduled conventions were cancelled; television documentaries of Chicago's decadence were produced; and politicians, both Democrat and Republican, assailed Daley's tactics. Democrat Abner Mikva, then candidate for Congress in Chicago's Second District, said, "The loss in business, the loss in prestige, the ridicule to which we have been and will be put have hurt a great deal."[12]

The mayor's counterattack to the defamation of his and Chicago's character was in the best tradition of the crusading politician. In rapid-fire succession, Daley answered his critics with facts and figures delivered in a style replete with malapropisms and "dis" and "dat."

```
". . . what about human bites?" he asked.  "What
have you heard about human bites, biting policemen,
taking part of their flesh out of their legs?  And
it was reported in the medium [sic] that this was
police brutality, the man had his teeth sunk into
the calf of the policeman, and the policeman was
trying to get him off.  What would you do, if some-
one was biting you?  Would you stand there calm and
collected and say go ahead, take another bite?"[13]
```

Daley followed the press conference by distributing his own White Paper in staunch defense of the Chicago police force. The details of the demonstrators' weapons were luridly catalogued as "glass ash trays," "live black widow spiders," "potatoes with razors hidden inside," "aerosol cans with contents which act as stink bombs," "knives and stilettos." The mayor's press conference and White Paper were carried in nearly every communication outlet in the United States, forcing his critics to countercharge, and thus keep the event alive in the media.

The mayor then assaulted his critics through the medium of television. He prepared an hour-long program defending the Chicago police. The presentation, though quite wooden, showed a moon-faced Daley enumerating the facts of the battle, as he saw them. He claimed that 198 policemen were injured, in comparison to "approximately" 60 civilians. The city of Chicago was portrayed as the last bastion of law and order in America. The mayor supported his film by appearing on "Meet the Press," "Face the Nation," and a half dozen other television programs to "tell the Chicago side of the story."

And then, not surprisingly, a ground swell of support sprang up for the mayor. Stories began to appear—stories reassessing the emotional events of late August: "Chicago's Durable Mayor," "Daley City Under Siege," "The King Richard Version," "Police State or Model City?" In these criticisms leveled at the mayor, the mayor's excesses at the convention were usually balanced with an account of his achievements—high-rise apartments, new industry, eight-lane expressways, and lighted alleys. And, above all, one fact was indisputable: Daley never would have received this publicity if it had not been for the head-cracking at the Convention.

Richard Daley excels in countering dissent with such ferocity and self-righteousness that public acclaim soon follows. Posing as one who vigilantly and vigorously seeks out injustices, the courageous crusader fights assassins of law and order. This strategy has been executed with success by others, including S. I. Hayakawa as president of San Francisco State, Samuel Yorty as mayor of Los Angeles, and Spiro T. Agnew as Vice-President of the United States. In each case, there is enough evidence to support the conclusion that protecting the public against dissent is both a convenient and a successful way to make it.

Norman—Abbie—Richard

There is little doubt that the subjects of these three case studies have made it in dissent. They may find themselves on opposite sides of the political fence, but this matters little. It takes a certain amount of ambition, guile, and persistence to make it in a business as competitive as revolution. The competition is fierce, and only those who are aware of the shifting patterns and alliances can survive.

Chicago Today   The People Talk   January 2, 1970

Jesus a revolutionary?

Billy Graham has made a statement that Jesus was a revolutionary.

I read my Bible and have found nothing in it to indicate this. I found Jesus, our beloved Lord, to be just what He was and is, "the Son of God, Who suffered and died for our salvation."

What on earth is wrong with the religious leaders of today? In one breath they preach "peace on earth," and in the next they are talking of revolution.

J. N.

14 How I Raised Myself to Position and Power Through Blockbusting

---

```
┌─────────────────────────────────────────┐
│  R-55    REAL ESTATE WANTED              │
│                                          │
│           START PACKING!                 │
│      LIST YOUR PROPERTY WITH             │
│               JING                       │
│      1891 N. CEDAR    VI 8-1285          │
│                                          │
│      GOOD REFERRAL BUYERS                │
│             WAITING                      │
│          FAST FINANCING                  │
│        GUARANTEED RESULTS                │
│             VI 8-1285                    │
│  ─────────────────────────────────      │
│     CASH FOR YOUR SOUTHSIDE              │
│             PROPERTY                     │
│        HOUSES OR 2 FLATS                 │
│      FAST DEAL    MR. BROWN              │
│            OR 2-1320                      │
└─────────────────────────────────────────┘
```

One of the most profitable businesses since World War II has been block-busting. Realtors move into an all-white neighborhood which adjoins a black ghetto and—through a number of strategies—panic the homeowners into selling cheaply. The enterprising realtors then resell the bargain-bought homes to blacks at inflated prices.

On the "racially changing" West Side of Chicago, an elderly woman sold her duplex, valued at $17,500, to a door-to-door real estate agent for $3300. The next day, the agent resold the duplex to a young black couple for $22,300—a profit of $19,000. The former homeowner took her case to court, claiming that the agent told her that he was doing her a favor "because as soon as the niggers move in, you'll be beaten, maimed, and raped." She lost the case. The elderly woman and countless other homeowners, both black and white, have been bilked of millions of dollars by the blockbuster—a sociological manipulator who masquerades as a real estate agent.

James Tinsley and Vast "Morizon"

The Morizon Realty Company is a highly specialized firm dealing in what James Tinsley, president, calls "preventive tensions in potentially explosive neighborhoods."

"Let's face it," says Tinsley, "these neighborhoods are going to change anyway. Why not get the whites out quickly and without bloodshed?" When I mentioned the enormous profit for the real estate companies in this venture, he looked appalled. "Listen! Anyone deserves to make a buck when a risk is involved. What if I can't 'turn' the property? I'm stuck with a mortgage and a high interest rate."

Tinsley did not bother to add that, in the ten years since opening Morizon, he has built a $150,000 home in the suburbs, owns a Mercedes, a Cadillac, and a Mustang, and has toured Europe, India, and South America on extended vacations.

Is Tinsley blockbusting in Argentina?

How did Jim make it?

The Phone Caller

To Tinsley, the most important communication instrument ever invented is the telephone. It is the telephone which allows his legion of terrorists to canvass a neighborhood in less than two days, and flush out any queasy homeowners. Tinsley prefers women to do his phone calling, because "they sound less hostile to the prospective client." Surprisingly, most of his callers are women whose homes have been blockbusted. "I guess they know a good deal when they see one," said Tinsley. "From any sale that results from one of their telephone contacts, they get 15 percent of the net profit."

Too often I've seen the have-nots turn into haves and become just as crummy as the haves they used to envy. Some of the fruit ranchers in California steam around in Cadillacs and treat the Mexican-American

field hands like vermin. Know who those bastards
are? They're the characters who rode west in
Steinbeck's trucks, in The Grapes of Wrath.

--Saul Alinsky[1]

Morizon's phone callers execute two strategies, both of which are highly
successful. In order to make sure that these strategies are used and used
properly, Tinsley posts a list of them all about the bullpen[*] and records all
the phone calls. The simplest is the "Sorry, Wrong Number" strategy:

"Mrs. Henry? How are you? This is Laura Ralston of Morizon Realty
calling about the sale of your house."

"I'm sorry, but you must be mistaken. My house isn't for sale."

"Oh, I thought with the Jenkins family moving in . . ." (or) "I thought
with the neighborhood becoming mixed . . ."

"Who are the Jenkins?" (or) "It is?"

"The colored people who bought the Smith home." (or) "It will be all
colored in three months. Do you want to be the only white family left in
the neighborhood?" (The number of whites who want to be the only ones
in a black neighborhood is miniscule.)

[*]A bullpen is a large room with phones and desks where sales personnel make their
calls.

This strategy, which is rooted in fear, is couched in the language and inflection of the chatty neighbor. The telephone solicitor is merely reporting gossip and in no obvious way trying to force a sale. All the assumptions will be made by the homeowner.

The second strategy, while still playing upon the subconscious fears of the homeowner, has the added inducement of greed. The caller dangles the word "cash" before the homeowner's mind and lets him conjure his own inflated notion as to how *much*. Some Morizon callers, in chatting with their intended victims, claim to have a home buyer with cash in hand. If the homeowner hesitates, he will lose the opportunity to sell, since the buyer purportedly has his eye on another home also. Actually, no buyer exists, but once the real estate agent has the property, he can do with it what he pleases. Usually, the agent waits to snare a home buyer who does not have enough money to make an adequate down payment, but who will pay an inflated price if he can be financed. Often such a buyer, if he can be assured of getting into the house immediately, will pay a premium ranging from $2000 to $3000 over the life of the mortgage. The proposition is especially attractive if the house is in a "nice" neighborhood.

The utility of the quick cash offer is that it adroitly eliminates the question of prejudice and fear for both the seller and the buyer. In most communities there are laws against panicking homeowners. Making a homeowner a cash offer for his property violates no laws; nevertheless all parties clearly understand the true intent of the phone call.

The cash deal affords the seller the benefit of not having to recite or rationalize his fears publicly. Most people like to maintain some illusions about their courage and unwillingness to abandon "a friendly, convenient-to-downtown neighborhood" threatened by a hostile invasion.

I like it here, mister.
I got a gun.
Screw the niggers.
Bricks fire lead.
No one pushes me around.

The Foot Soldier

When a neighborhood begins to panic, there is an endless sea of For Sale signs along the streets. The door-to-door real estate agent is the man who orchestrates the symphony of these signs. He travels up and down neighborhoods probing for homeowners who might succumb to the panic (initiated by the phone caller) and sell. Acting in concert with a phone lead or noting an aged couple tending roses in their yard, the realtor approaches his intended victims with an arsenal of strategies calculated to play upon their fears and prejudices.

"The good agent studies his client as a chess master studies his board," claims Tinsley. "He analyzes the situation carefully and then decides upon his move. The agent has to have some kind of door-opener. He can't knock on someone's door and, when they answer, yell, 'The niggers are coming!' There are laws against that sort of thing. Besides, I'm not running an anti-minority-group operation. What the agent has to do is to create a situation in which the buyer initiates the proposal to sell."

A number of strategies enable the door-to-door agent to mask his real purpose. A favorite opener is for the agent to ring the doorbell while he is in an apparent state of hysteria. Under the homeowner's questioning, the agent reveals he was assaulted by a gang of black toughs only two blocks away. While being calmed by the homeowner, the agent waits for the anticipated lament of "What's this neighborhood coming to?" This is the cue for the agent to reveal that he happens to be associated with a real estate agency. The sympathetic relationship already nurtured by the purported assault makes it natural for the homeowner to list with the realtor's company. It is as if fate has thrown the two parties together.

Self-Presentation Hints

1. Clients judge you by the car you drive. We require a full-size car no older than two years. Keep it clean.
2. Buy good, well-fitting suits of medium price (Botany 500, Eagle). The best colors are greens and browns which are friendly, but not somber. No Edwardian suits, Italian shoes, or English ascots. Look like any respectable professional man.
3. Carry yourself in a confident manner. But do not appear boastful. Do not walk on people's lawns or spit on their sidewalks.

—Morizon Realty

Acting the Good Samaritan is also an effective ruse for entering a house. Supposedly, an unnamed friend is concerned for the homeowner's safety and welfare and has asked the agent to stop in and see how the homeowner and his family are doing. Or, neighbors down the block are planning on evacuating, and they thought the Horgesheimers also might be ready to move. The loopholes in this strategy can be closed easily. When pressed as to the informant's identity, the agent pleads confidentiality because of ethics. Few people will challenge the motives of a man piously pleading ethics.

```
I still stand by the testimony I gave before the
U.S. Civil Rights Commission five years ago.  Then
I defined a racially integrated community as a
chronological term timed from the entrance of the
first black family to the exit of the last white
family.  While the blacks are moving in and the
whites are moving out it's integrated.
```
--Saul Alinsky[2]

Money

If the homeowner can resist the pressure of Tinsley's sales personnel and delays selling for one year after a neighborhood panic-selling campaign, he stands a good chance of being able to sell his home at full value—if he wants to. Tinsley knows this fact, and it reinforces the urgency of sweeping the neighborhood clean of whites.

James Tinsley's Remarks to New Sales Personnel

"This is the best business in the world. It beats being a doctor, lawyer, or Injun chief. We scare the hell out of a bunch of old ladies, Polacks, Yids, and Micks. We buy their houses for ten cents on a dollar and make a thousand percent on resale. It is not crooked, and no one goes to jail. There is nothing immoral about it—they're going to move, anyway. If you don't get to them, someone else will. If you're any good, you'll be working for yourself inside of a year. This is too good a racket to work for someone else."

15 The Country Hustle

John Rondy runs the Rush Lake Ballroom, which is situated 180 miles northwest of Minneapolis. The ballroom is nestled at a point equidistant from the villages of New York Mills (population 937), Henning (population 848), and Eagle Bend (population 650). On Saturday nights during the summer season, the ballroom is open for the enjoyment of the local youths, the farmers, and the vacationers. The evening when I visited, Albert Tschkash's (Zi-KISH) Band was playing, and the place was jammed with people—750 of them, to be exact.

Rondy, the owner and entrepreneur, occupies the cabin next to the ballroom; and on this particular evening, he was crouched on the bed, counting his revenue. At $1.50 per head, he was doing all right. Tschkash's five-piece band costs Rondy only $325; the turkey farmer who takes tickets, $10; four bartenders, $12.50 each; and the waitresses, the government minimum of $1.60. Rondy charges 25 cents for set-ups, and 50 cents for a beer. The former management used to pour a pitcher of mix or beer for 50 cents, but Rondy discontinued the practice as bad business. If a customer sneaks into the rest room and adds tap water to the mix, he quickly discovers that his drink has turned a snuff color brown: Rondy is blessed with high-mineral-content water in his taps. He has never found it economically desirable to add a water softener.

For four hours of entertainment a week, John Rondy makes between three and four thousand dollars. The strategies he uses to mold Rush Lake into a money-making operation are worth study.

Upon entering Rondy's Ballroom, one's attention is immediately attracted to the hundreds of strips of tinsel, in every color of the rainbow, hung rakishly from the rafters. Red, green, and blue balloons attached to all the tables lend an air of festivity. Rondy says the other dance halls don't have these little frills, which, half joking, he claims bring in $100 for every strip of tinsel.

The music is strictly pre-1960. Tschkash mixes polkas and schottisches with country-and-western tunes such as "Cold, Cold Heart" and "Big Bad John," and adds such standards as "Tea for Two" and "Slow Boat to China." All of Tschkash's renditions sound alike, with a heavy tuba beat and a lack of rhythm and tone.

To say that Tschkash is a second-rate Lawrence Welk would not be fair. Albert Tschkash is king in northwest Minnesota. His band members wear midnight-blue jackets highlighted with silver lamé thread. The pants are black, and taper to pointed black leather shoes which glint in the spotlight. (When things got bad for the big bands in the fifties, their old outfits were sold through mail-order ads.) Every time Tschkash meets a visitor from Minneapolis, he asks him what band leader had the initials *T. D.* Tschkash sings and plays an accordion. He is best on the "box" with foot-stompin', old-time polkas, and is much less effective when he croons "Your Cheating Heart" in an attempt to imitate Eddy Arnold. The rest of the Tschkash band changes personnel from year to year. Now, a tall kid on the bass fiddle plays first saxophone in the Sebeka High School Band. Tschkash's tuba player is an alcoholic from Zumbrota, Minnesota, who claimed he once played for the King of Polka, Whoopee John Wilfahrt. The guitarist is Tschkash's cousin, and the clarinetist owned and operated a village theater until business fell off. Together, the five produce "the Tschkash sound," which one music critic from Fargo, North Dakota, dubbed "an elephant fighting a thousand mockingbirds."

The dancers do not seem to mind the critic's assessment as they swirl

about, fox-trotting, lindy-hopping, twisting, bunny-hopping, or doing whatever other step they know best. It helps to be brawny because couples
enthusiastically bang into each other on the crowded dance floor. The
tight corner under the suspended electric fan is particularly treacherous.
Frequently, women dance together, but no one seems to mind. In the
country, farmers are tired after working in the fields, and the wives like to
dance. The result of the individual dance styles is in sharp contrast to what
could be expected to happen, for example, at a Rolling Stone Concert in
Los Angeles in the year 1969:

The place exploded. It was as if someone had cried
fire or abandon ship; they jumped walls, leaped
over chairs, shoved or belted anyone who had the
misfortune to get in the way, and dropped ten feet
from the balcony.[1]

The scene at Rondy's is as if time had been frozen in 1955. No one
wears sideburns, bell bottoms, or smokes pot. No one is into acid rock,
revolution, or alienation. The Middle East, blacks, and pollution are all part
of another world which barely reaches the area through the one local TV
station. Rondy's roisterers drink a lot of hard liquor and local beer and keep
the restrooms full. In this rarefied atmosphere, John Rondy obviously is
making it.

Making It in the Country

Tonight, the band members, having completed a set of "Tennessee Waltz,"
"Smoke Gets in Your Eyes," "Mockingbird Hill," and two polkas, scramble
for the bar. Rondy enters the ballroom wearing an ill-fitting toast-colored
suit (a little rumpled from kneeling on the bed and counting his take) and a
string tie, set off by a plaid shirt and a gold watch fob. After greeting a
number of customers with handshakes, congenial jabs to the arm, and
knowing winks, he explains his philosophy of running a ballroom to me:

"If the music is rock or some of the raunchy blues," says Rondy, "the
customer will either get mad or stop drinking. Either way, I lose. I play old
standards—the same every Saturday night. It's nice and regular. The people
know that at five minutes to 12:00 the band plays 'Show Me the Way to Go
Home' and, at the stroke of midnight, 'Goodnight, Sweetheart.' These are
good people. They come to let off a little steam and drink a little."

Among the appeals of his Rush Lake Ballroom, Rondy lists on his
posters:

CENTRALLY LOCATED
HEATED
INDOOR TOILETS
A CLEAN PLACE
SEE YOUR FRIENDS
LOTS OF PARKING
THIS IS WHERE THE ACTION IS!

"I work this place hard. Every Monday morning, I distribute posters all over the area. I have regular stops where I give free tickets in exchange for displaying the posters—barber shops, bars, VFW clubs, theaters—you name it. There are sixteen dance halls within twenty miles of here. *Their* owners are sleeping off a drunk while I'm working as far west as Long Prairie, getting out my advertisements.

"Crestview Lodge is a nice place; but if you have to go to the bathroom, you use an outhouse—rain, snow, tornado. Did you ever use an outhouse at eleven o'clock at night, half-potted, and flies snapping at you? The first thing I did was put in modern plumbing."

Rondy has one tactic unique to the area: He selects an item to huckster at the dance. About 10:30, he mounts the stage and delivers the message. Last week it was a thirty-selection, memorial record album of top country-and-western hits by an unknown named Krinkle. "I got the records from a jobber in Minneapolis for 75 cents apiece. They bought 'em for a late-night-movie promotion, and it flopped. At $3.95, I moved a hundred, and could've sold *five* hundred." Rondy claims that the important element in selling novelties is maintaining the uniqueness and scarcity of the product. His pitch that evening was brief and effective:

```
"I've got here a special promotion from a major
record company. [Lie]  Give me a minute, will you!
[Sympathy appeal]  This album ordinarily sells for
$25.  [Big lie]  But I'm going to give them away
tonight.  [Now they'll listen!]  All of the great
country songs of the fifties are on this album.
[Exaggeration]  'Sixteen Tons,' 'Slow Poke'--you
name it, it's here.  [Identification]  All are sung
by one of the great, young, clean, Nashville singing
stars.  [Who's to know?]  Now I'd love to give them
away [equivocation], but the record manufacturer
wanted to be sure that only sincere people who will
enjoy the records will receive them.  [Flattery]  So
I am authorized by the company to allow each head of
a family to purchase one record, and one record only,
for $3.95."  [They'll lie and cheat to get more
than one.]
```

GOD LOVES A PROMOTER
—Marty Robbins, Country western singer[2]

Tonight Rondy shilled cigarette lighters, "embossed with Big Ten football coaches' pictures in rich color. Collectors' items that will be worth a fortune in ten years. I have only forty."

Rondy can remember only one promotion that did not make it. He once bought one million straight pins at an incredibly low price, and they are still in his basement. "I even investigated having miniature pictures of Grand Ole Opry stars on the head; but at the time, it wasn't technically possible."

Rules of the House

NO SPITTING ON FLOOR.
NO ONE UNDER EIGHTEEN ADMITTED.
NO FIGHTING.
NO SPANISH FLY.
NO BRINGING OWN BEER.
NO ADMISSION WITHOUT TICKET.
HAVE A GOOD TIME!

—JOHN RONDY

"Running a ballroom is a rough business. You have to run a tight ship. I hire a cop for $25 a night to keep the peace. Sure, there's underage kids drinking. But if I throw them out, they'd just go down the road and take their overage friends with them.

"There's a lot of high-class people who think I'm some kind of devil for running a ballroom. I know they cheat and steal six days a week, and then play Holy Joe on Sunday. They never come here; they have their phony country clubs and 'state' dinners. Last week some WCTUs [Women's Christian Temperance Union] from Frazee came down and told me to close up. One of them said I'd go to hell for leading kids to debauchery. That's why I have rules! One Saturday-night brawl, and every kooky, Bible-belting son-of-a-bitch newspaper editor in the county would write an editorial. You've got to stay low profile in the country."

Roller Skating
Snowmobiling
Florida

"In the winter, when I go to Florida, I rent the ballroom to a guy who puts on roller skating three nights a week. The rest of the week, snow-mobilers stop in for beer during nighttime rides."

The Country Hustler: Credentials

SON OF CARPET LAYER
SIXTH-GRADE EDUCATION
PFC, PACIFIC THEATER
BRICKLAYER
FARMER
GAS STATION OPERATOR
BALLROOM PROPRIETOR

"In 1952, I bought this place for $5000 and $750 down. The owner and his wife had separated and the bank had taken it over. This year, the net profit will be $100,000 after expenses. I like to think it's because this is a well-run operation.

"I don't have to pay a band like Tschkash $325. I can get some local kids for half that. But why be cheap? You only hurt the operation. It's like the pizza operator trying to cut his preparation cost from 32 cents to 28 cents by using cheaper tomato sauce on a pizza he gets $3.00 for. Give the customer the best. Once a year, I get Whoopee John and pay him a thousand dollars. People say, 'Wow, Whoopee John!' and associate your place with a first-class operation. Whoopee John is a loss leader. Just like A&P buys AA butter for 82-1/2 cents a pound and sells it to the public for 79 cents. It keeps the crowd coming—and, meantime, they make a mint by boosting the price on a lot of other things.

"Do you like that tap beer? That's Budweiser. I could use local stuff in that spigot. I use Bud. You know why? Because people like to go first class. The mix is Canada Dry. The best. Always give them the best. The toilet paper is Scott. Glassware by Anchor. Chairs by American Seating— cushioned. Some dance halls buy chairs at church auctions. You asked me my philosophy? Give 'em the best."

Conclusion:
There They Go Again

The techniques of manipulation are bound to change. Instead of put-ons, there might be on-puts, and avoidance may replace confrontation. Some new and clear patterns of manipulation will surface in the seventies.

1. The struggle to control media will be accentuated with repercussions in the classroom. For example, instruction in public speaking courses will no longer emphasize heavily the making of speeches as such, but will teach strategies of getting the student on media in order to make a speech.

2. Consumer protection laws will make the obvious, small-time manipulators such as car salesmen extinct. Standardized prices will protect the buyer, but will subtract some of the joy from the strategy of buying. Large-

scale graft such as stock manipulation will be greater. Media will enable manipulators to swindle all over the world without actually being there in person. A Barney Jullip selling mutual funds on worldwide television is not too far distant in time.

3. Major battles will be fought for control of media rather than for land. There wi.. be an increasing use of media for special-interest purposes. Groups wishing to organize for politics, fellowship, or community-action will attempt to buy FM radio or UHF television stations as naturally as they used to buy uniforms for a softball or bowling team. Public relations experts will be retrained to serve as media advisers to manage accounts for such small groups as Rotary Clubs and John Birch Societies.

4. The clanging will not stop, but there will be counter-clanging devices. Automatic hearing instruments will selectively screen all clanging.

5. In the long run, the media which enabled minorities to grab for power will frustrate them. The spectacle of Operation Breadbasket's being challenged as unegalitarian by WASPs may not be far off.

6. The Establishment will go into arts with a zest and a determination without precedent in world history. In the next decade, both governments and businesses will try to buy off the artists. The artist will be seen as the foremost hindrance to mass manipulation, and the Establishment will try to incorporate the creative people into the corporate framework. There is already indication that this is beginning to happen. Rock groups are becoming controlled by syndicates who supervise material and purge recalcitrant musicians. The record industry and tape industry will continue the process of gathering and devouring the small companies, a process which will eventually freeze out the innovative performer.

7. The desire for interpersonal relationships through such means as the Esalen Institute will continue as a national pastime. People will become so locked into the clanging and the artificiality of media that they will seek encounters with real people. The back porch will become institutionalized by systematic encounter groups all over the country.

These projections make up only a small portion of the future of communication. Although the emphasis in this book has been upon a number of communicative strategies and forms, it is important to recognize that these examples do not represent a complete set. Most modern human communication, whether personal or mass, is manipulative. The co-ed who tries to "shake down" her father for some money by dressing "straight" is just as manipulative as Barney Jullip, the car salesman. And as long as people concentrate on the kind of communication that is evaluated by its impact rather than its promotion of understanding, there will be little change in manipulative practices.

An important change in our manipulative society would be to concentrate on communication which strengthens rather than weakens the system. There are a number of trends which reflect an attempt to build this positive communication. Providing consumers with information on strategies of deception is one obvious attempt to equalize communication power, and this approach has been the focus of this book. Sensitivity and encounter groups, though sometimes abused, are other approaches to building a stronger communication system. Though consumer information and group work may produce only piecemeal changes in the reshifting of the communication system, still they are optimistic developments. The only alternatives to these attempts may be to scrap our existing communication system and begin anew. This process may have started already.

Notes

Introduction

[1] Joe Cappo, "Tape Vending Machine Foils Sticky Fingers," *Chicago Daily News,* August 28, 1970, p. 45.
[2] *Chicago Daily News*, August 28, 1970, p. 45.

Chapter 1

[1] Jacob Brackman, "Onward and Upward with the Arts," *New Yorker* (June 24, 1970): 34. I am indebted to Mr. Brackman for giving me the idea that led to the writing of this chapter.
[2] Ibid., p. 73.
[3] Studs Terkel, *Hard Times* (New York: Avon Books, 1971), p. 225.
[4] Joseph Gelmis, *The Film Director as Superstar* (Garden City, N.Y.: Doubleday & Company, Inc., 1970), p. 50.

Chapter 2

[1] John Sinclair, "Message to the People of Woodstock Nation," *Sun Dance* 1(July 4, 1970): 7.
[2] Lewis Carroll, *Complete Works of Lewis Carroll* (New York: Random House, Inc., 1936), p. 214.
[3] Arthur L. Smith, *Rhetoric of Black Revolution* (Boston: Allyn & Bacon, Inc., 1969), p. 19.
[4] Joe McGinniss, *The Selling of the President, 1968* (New York: Trident Press, 1969), p. 237.
[5] Ibid., p. 206.
[6] Ibid., pp. 73-74.
[7] Ibid., p. 37.

Chapter 3

[1] Eldridge Cleaver, "The White Race and Its Heroes." In *Soul on Ice* (New York: Dell Publishing Co., Inc., 1968), p. 70.

Chapter 4

[1] "The Tactic: Confrontation/The Aim: Disruption," *Life*, October 18, 1968, p. 77.
[2] Lawrence E. Eichel et al., *The Harvard Strike* (Boston: Houghton Mifflin Company, 1970), p. 102.
[3] Norman F. Cantor, *The Age of Protest* (New York: Hawthorn Books, Inc., 1969), p. 303.
[4] John R. Searle, "A Foolproof Scenario for Student Revolts," *The New York Times Magazine* (December 29, 1968): 12.
[5] James Forman, "Manifesto to White Christian Churches and Jewish Synagogues" (Speech delivered to the Board Meeting of the National Council of Churches, New York City, May 2, 1969).
[6] *Indiana: The Anatomy of Violence*, a report prepared by The Faculty Committee to Investigate the Dow Incident at Indiana University. In *Protest: Student Activism in America*, ed. Julian Foster and Durwood Long (New York: William Morrow & Co., Inc., 1970), p. 241.
[7] Adolf Hitler, as quoted in Jerome Beatty, Jr., "Trade Winds," *Saturday Review* (May 17, 1969): 10.
[8] Public Safety Commissioner Leo Laughlin, as quoted in *The Boston Globe*, April 10, 1969, p. 39.

[9] Eichel et al., *The Harvard Strike*, p. 324.

[10] James S. Turner, "Ohio State: Free Speech and Student Power." In *Protest: Student Activism in America*, ed. Foster and Long, p. 353.

[11] Kurt Vonnegut, Jr., *Player Piano* (New York: Avon Books, 1967), p. 296.

Chapter 5

[1] Jerry L. Avorn et al., *Up Against the Ivy Wall* (New York: Atheneum Publishers, 1968), p. 292.

[2] Ashley Montagu, *The Anatomy of Swearing* (New York: The Macmillan Company, 1967), p. 105.

[3] Robert L. Scott, "The Rhetoric of Student Unrest" (Paper delivered at the Convention of the Central States Speech Association, St. Louis, Mo., April 18, 1969), pp. 9-10.

[4] "D***T: A Parable," *Peace and Freedom News* (Baltimore Md.), May 23, 1968.

[5] Speech delivered at the Harvard Commencement, Cambridge, Mass., June 12, 1969.

[6] From an anonymous handbill distributed at Harvard University, Cambridge, Mass., April 1969.

[7] Roger Kahn, *The Battle for Morningside Heights: Why Students Rebel* (New York: William Morrow & Co., Inc., 1970), p. 204.

[8] Ibid.

[9] John Cohn, ed., *The Essential Lenny Bruce* (New York: Ballantine Books, Inc., 1970), p. 232.

[10] William F. Buckley, Jr., *The Unmaking of a Mayor* (New York: Bantam Books, Inc., 1967), p. 149.

[11] Ethel Grodzins Romm, *The Open Conspiracy* (New York: Avon Books, 1971), p. 41.

[12] Ibid.

[13] "Middle America's Mr. America," *Newsweek*, September 28, 1970, p. 26.

Chapter 6

[1] Kenneth Keniston, *Young Radicals* (New York: Harcourt Brace Jovanovich, Inc., 1968), Chapter 8.

[2] Michael Novak, "End of Ideology?" *Commonweal* 87(March 8, 1968): 680.

How They Did It

[1] Paul Senn, *The Lawless Decade* (New York: Crown Publishers, Inc., 1957), p. 214.

[2] Irving J. Tressler, *How to Lose Friends and Alienate People* (New York: Stackpole Books, 1937), p. 55.

[3] Maulana Ron Karenga, "The Portable Karenga." In *The Black Revolt*, ed. Floyd B. Barbour (New York: P. F. Collier, Inc., 1968), p. 192.

[4] Bernard Malamud, *The Natural* (New York: Dell Publishing Co., Inc., 1969), p. 172.

[5] Ned Polsky, *Hustlers, Beats, and Others* (New York: Doubleday Anchor Books, 1969), p. 96.

[6] Paraphrased in Robert Townsend, *Up the Organization* (New York: Random House, Inc., 1970), p. 162.

Chapter 7

[1] Jonathan Eisen, ed., Preface to *The Age of Rock* (New York: Random House, Inc., 1969), p. xv.

[2] Robert Lipsyte, "You Gits a Little Uppity and You Lands in Jail," *Esquire* (August 1967); 75.

Chapter 8

[1] Richard Wright, Foreword to *The Meaning of the Blues*, by Paul Oliver (New York: P. F. Collier, Inc., 1960), p. 10.
[2] Paul Oliver, *The Meaning of the Blues* (New York: P. F. Collier, Inc., 1960), p. 332.
[3] Stefan Grossman, *Ragtime Blues Guitarists* (New York: Oak Publishing Co., 1970), p. 80.
[4] Harry Oster, *Living Country Blues* (Detroit: Folklore Associates, 1969), p. 376.
[5] Jones, *Blues People*, p. 145.
[6] "Chicken Soup Freak," *Time*, February 28, 1969, p. 53.
[7] Oliver, *The Meaning of the Blues*, p. 196.
[8] Oster, *Living Country Blues*, p. 439.
[9] Charles Keil, *Urban Blues* (Chicago: University of Chicago Press, 1966), p. 181.
[10] "Living Blues," *Chicago* 2(Summer 1970): 7.

Chapter 9

[1] "Getting the Business" (Interview with Max Cooperstein, former national promotion manager of Chess Record Company), *Chicago Seed*, 5(10): 14.
[2] Robert Rosenstone, "The Times They Are A-Changin'," *The Music of Protest: The Annals of the American Academy*, March 1969, p. 114.
[3] Harry Shearer, "Captain Pimple Cream's Fiendish Plot." In *The Age of Rock*, ed. Jonathan Eisen (New York: Random House, Inc., 1969), p. 368.
[4] Alvin Toffler, "The Future as a Way of Life." In *Worlds in the Making*, ed. Mary Jane Dunstan and Patricia W. Harlan (Englewood Cliffs, N.J.: Prentice-Hall, Inc., 1970), p. 1.

Chapter 10

[1] Roger Daniels and Harry Kitano, *American Racism* (Englewood Cliffs, N.J.: Prentice-Hall, Inc., 1970), p. 108.
[2] Parker Tyler, *Magic and Myth of the Movies* (New York: Simon and Schuster, Inc., 1947), preface.
[3] Ibid., p. 158.
[4] David Manning White, ed., *Pop Culture in America* (Chicago: Quadrangle Books, Inc., 1970), p. 3.
[5] Richard Gilman, "1 + 1," *Partisan Review* 2(1970): 277.

Chapter 11

[1] John Ciardi, "Manner of Speaking," *Saturday Review* (May 16, 1970): 10.

How It Proliferates

[1] Antonin Artaud, "No More Masterpieces." In *The American Experience: A Radical Reader*, ed. Harold Jaffe and John Tytell (New York: Harper & Row, Publishers, 1970), pp. 306-307.
[2] Elizabeth Campbell, "Rolling Stone Raps with Peter Fonda." In *Easy Rider*, by Peter Fonda et al. (New York: New American Library, Signet Edition, 1969), p. 32.

[3] Chester Himes, *Hot Day, Hot Night* (New York: Dell Publishing Co., Inc., 1969), p. 137.

[4] Marshall McLuhan, *McLuhan: Hot and Cool* (New York: New American Library, Signet Edition, 1967), p. 119.

[5] Dennis Hopper, with L. M. Kit Carson, "Hopper," *Moderator,* December 1969, p. 18.

[6] Chester Anderson, "Notes for the New Geology." In *Notes for the New Underground*, ed. Jesse Kornbluth (New York: Ace Publishing Corp., 1968), pp. 78-79.

[7] LeRoi Jones, "The Revolutionary Theatre." In *The American Experience: A Radical Reader*, ed. Jaffe and Tytell, p. 93.

Chapter 13

[1] Daniel and Gabriel Cohn-Bendit, *Obsolete Communism: The Left Wing Alternative*, trans. Arnold Pomerans (New York: McGraw-Hill Book Company, 1968).

[2] James Toback, "At Play in the Fields of the Bored," *Esquire* 70(December 1968): 155.

[3] "Flying High with Mailer," *Newsweek,* December 9, 1968, p. 86.

[4] Ibid., pp. 84-88.

[5] Toback, "At Play in the Fields of the Bored," p. 152.

[6] See "Flying High with Mailer," pp. 84-88; and Norman Mailer, *Advertisements for Myself* (New York: G. P. Putnam's Sons, A Berkley Medallion Book, 1966), pp. 203, 215-216, 221, 227.

[7] Jane O'Reilly, "Diary of a Mailer Trailer." In *Running Against the Machine*, ed. Peter Manso (Garden City, N.Y.: Doubleday & Company, Inc., 1969), p. 283.

[8] Abbie Hoffman, *Revolution for the Hell of It* (New York: The Dial Press, 1968), p. 203.

[9] Ibid., p. 49.

[10] "King Richard Version," *Newsweek*, September 23, 1968, p. 35.

[11] See *Reader's Guide to Periodical Literature*, 27(March 1967 to February 1968), and 28(March 1968 to February 1969).

[12] Raymond R. Coffey, "Dossier on Daley," *Nation* 207(October 7, 1968): 331.

[13] "King Richard Version," p. 35.

Chapter 14

[1] Marion Sanders, *The Professional Radical: Conversations with Saul Alinsky* (New York: Harper & Row, Publishers, Perennial Library, 1970), p. 53.

[2] Ibid., p. 86.

Chapter 15

[1] Jerry Hopkins, "Kiss Kiss Flutter Flutter Thank You Thank You," *Rolling Stone* 48(December 13, 1969): 6.

[2] Larry L. King, "The Grand Old Opry," *Harper's Magazine* 237(July 1968): 50.

"Things" You'll Want to Read

Abrahams, Roger D. *Positively Black*. Englewood Cliffs, N.J.: Prentice-Hall, Inc., 1970. A folklorist's collection and analysis of black literature and communication. See especially the section entitled "Men of Words," page 37.

Agel, Jerome, ed. *The Making of Kubrick's 2001*. New York: New American Library, Signet Edition, 1970. The rhetoric of a film comprehensively outlined. "If *2001* has stirred your emotions, your subconscious, your mythological yearnings, then it has succeeded."—Stanley Kubrick.

Cohn, John, ed. *The Essential Lenny Bruce*. New York: Ballantine Books, Inc., 1970. A collection of some of Bruce's finest material. The book gives excellent examples of the comedian as persuader.

DeTurk, David A., and A. Poulin, eds. *The American Folk Scene: Dimensions of the Folksong Revival*. New York: Dell Publishing Company, Laurel Edition, 1967. A good introduction to a typically non-researched area. There are provocative articles on Bob Dylan, Pete Seeger, and Woody Guthrie.

Edmund's New Car Prices. New York: Edmund Publication Corporation. Anyone who does not consult this guide before purchasing a car is deserving of the low ball. Once the price is settled, all you have to worry about is the rhetoric of the new car delivery: DENTS—STEERING FAILURES—BALLJOINT CRACKS—GAS TANK LEAKS—WERE THE BODY FRAME BOLTS TIGHTENED?

Eisen, Jonathan, ed. *The Age of Rock*. New York: Random House, Inc., 1969. A collection of essays on rock which are quite representative of the writing in the late sixties. Especially worth reading are the articles by H. F. Mooney, Robert Christgau, and Harry Shearer.

The Gulf Oil Walt Disney Comic Book. Mickey Mouse and Gulf Oil combine to provide the first credit-card comic book. The comics, though somewhat smudged by service station attendants, are bringing kids good, wholesome fun through the strategy of the point-of-purchase sale.

Jaffe, Harold, and John Tytell, eds. *The American Experience: A Radical Reader*. New York: Harper and Row, Publishers, 1970. An exciting collection of recent trends in American culture.

Keil, Charles. *Urban Blues*. Chicago: University of Chicago Press, 1967. The definitive study of the rhetoric of urban blues. Keil writes incisively with a wealth of background material and research. Especially rewarding is the concluding chapter which suggests profitable areas of blues investigation.

Manso, Peter, ed. *Running Against the Machine*. Garden City, N.Y.: Doubleday & Company, Inc., 1969. A collection of articles describing the Norman Mailer/Jimmy Breslin campaign for the New York mayoralty. Some of the ideas presented by the ticket: "A zoo in every neighborhood." "An effort will be made to return national baseball teams to Brooklyn and Manhattan." "Vegas East at Coney Island." Says Norman, "This is not my book, for I didn't write it and was not present to edit it, although I think the editing work is more than fair."

McGinnis, Joe. *The Selling of the President, 1968*. New York: Trident Press, 1969. This book has made a fortune for McGinnis—it must be good. Joe explains with brutal frankness how Richard M. Nixon was managed to the presidency through the use of television. Now, if Joe will tell us how he sold his book . . . .

Modern Romances. Dell Publishing Company. A magazine form directed at elderly women. In the typical true-confession format, the periodical reader has an opportunity to read all about "college chicks," "white briefs," and "icy hands." When the world seems complex, buy a copy and read about "fallen women," "sex fiends," "lovingly caressing," and "going farther." The discussions of "hot love" will remind you that many people are "like animals" and not "smooth" or "sophisticated."

Oliver, Paul. *The Meaning of the Blues.* New York: P. F. Collier, Inc., 1966. A valuable discography of the blues.

Podhoretz, Norman. *Making It.* New York: Bantam Books, Inc., 1969. A nice boy who made it in the literary establishment. Also a nice title!

Polsky, Ned. *Hustlers, Beats, and Others.* New York: Doubleday Anchor Books, 1969. An explanation of how to hustle at pool. Something any fledgling student who frequents student unions should know.

Roszak, Theodore. *The Making of a Counter Culture.* New York: Doubleday Anchor Books, 1969. An insightful account of the influence of technology on all aspects of culture. The chapter on "Technocracy's Children" establishes definitions that are much needed.

Sears and Roebuck Catalogue. Here is America's "finest" merchandise exhibited in Sears' clever understatement. "A truly fantastic low price for the famous Polaroid Big Swinger camera. Only $9.44." "Hand-finished statuary from Italy . . . including this replica of the Winged Victory, $23.99." "For the first time Sears offers a jacket and ski-mobile suit with electronic quilting." From the Sears "Ship-A-Gift" service to the Sears Deferred Easy Payment Plan, the latest in redefinition of products and services.

Shaffer, Ivan. *The Midas Compulsion.* New York: Dell Publishing Co., Inc., 1970. The fictive saga of Jackie—the kid who made it as a stock manipulator. A "schlock" novel which has a lot of sex and violence. What makes the book worth citing is the price—$1.25—and the fact that a large number of people bought it, which suggests SEX: "Gamy, lurid, more explicit sex than in *The Love Machine."—Publishers' Weekly*; or MONEY: "Taut play-by-play accounts of stock operations . . . tangled manipulations and financial intrigue . . . utterly fascinating."*—The New York Times*; or BOTH:"Sex and the stock market . . . the story of Jackie Greenstein, who wheels and deals in stocks and women."*—Dayton News Tribune.*

Shecter, Leonard. *The Jocks.* New York: Paperback Library, 1969. How to make it in sports. All about fixing fights, dumping baseball games, and shaving points in basketball. In this book, the fledgling jock learns that Michigan State once offered a B.S. degree with a major in mobile homes, and that many colleges offer credit in golf and ballroom dancing.

Shostrom, Everett L. *Man, the Manipulator.* New York: Bantam Books, Inc., 1968. Are you a "bully," "calculator," "nice guy," or "clinging vine"? Shostrom will relieve your anxieties by explaining how manipulators can move to actualization. This book, which, according to the publisher, "lets you in on some of your best-kept secrets!" is full of confessions. A good book for the person interested in manipulations and who likes movie magazines.

Swanberg, W. A. *Citizen Hearst.* New York: Bantam Matrix Edition, 1967. The biography of William Randolph Hearst, who really made it in rhetoric. He started wars, ran for President, and owned castles. He also loved a sled named "Rosebud."

Time Magazine. The first really put-on magazine devoted to news coverage. Rarely serious, this weekly magazine combines zany writing with mad-cap ideas. Their funniest put-on is the hilarious Man of the Year. Summary—a great magazine.

Toffler, Alvin. *Future Shock.* New York: Random House, Inc., 1970. According to Orville G. Brim, President of the Russell Sage Foundation, "*Future Shock* crackles with more insight into the nature of change in society than any book I have read in years." Even Marshall McLuhan claims "*Future Shock* by Alvin Toffler is 'where it's at.'" Now, any book which "crackles" and is also loved by McLuhan has to be read. Besides, Alvin needs the money.

Townsend, Robert. *Up the Organization.* New York: Alfred A. Knopf, Inc., 1970. Says the business bible, "And God created the organization and gave it dominion over man." Says Robert Townsend, "In my book any-

one who has an assistant-to should be fined a hundred dollars a day
until he eliminates the position." (p. 24.) Says Knopf, "*Up the Organization* . . . is the best, strongest, funniest, sagest, most outrageous and
constructive book ever written."

Williams, Heathcote. *The Speakers.* New York: Grove Press, Inc., 1966.
An excellent analysis of the speakers who frequent London's Hyde Park.
If you like speeches.